THE MAKING OF A MAN

By

ORISON SWETT MARDEN

Editor of "Success"

Author of "Stepping Stones," "Winning Out," "How They Succeeded," *etc.*

BOSTON ·.· LOTHROP
PUBLISHING COMPANY

Published, August, 1905

NORWOOD PRESS
BERWICK & SMITH CO.
NORWOOD, MASS.
U. S. A.

Kessinger Publishing's Rare Reprints
Thousands of Scarce and Hard-to-Find Books!

We kindly invite you to view our extensive catalog list at:
http://www.kessinger.net

CONTENTS

THE MAKING OF A MAN

CHAPTER I

THE MAKING OF A MAN

WHAT is a successful horse? The animal that develops his peculiar powers. To develop manliness is the goal to which every man is to be guided. Unless a book of advice leads one to Manhood, it is a blind guide.

"Human creatures are very plentiful," said Herodotus, "but men are very scarce."

What is manliness? What is a successful man? Is it not one of the first great lessons of life to make a just estimate of the value of one's activities? Does not true success in life depend largely upon this?

Do not refinement of spirit, breadth of sympathy, depth of insight, and a vast deal of round-about common-sense relating to life's business, pertain to success? If not, our race is most unfortunate.

Are not sincerity, the making good of what you promise, entire truthfulness of spirit, to be accounted in estimating true success? What is it but weighing wind, to call an unprincipled man successful?

The difference between man and the lower animals is a moral one. "The motives of conscience," says Darwin, "as connected with repentance and the feelings of duty, are the most important differences which separate man from the animal." This is but another way of saying what we read in the earliest record, that God made man in his own image.

When, therefore, we ask what is success, the answer is found along moral lines. A successful horse must be a pronounced success as a horse, in the development of the powers that differentiate him from other animals. And unless a man is well developed in his moral faculties, by which alone he is differentiated from other animals, he is not a success as a man.

A recently published letter of Gibbon, the historian, contains a significant reference to Charles James Fox, who had just paid him a visit at Lausanne. An enthusiastic description of the charm of Fox's conversation breaks off with a hint of scandal followed by a deeply regretful query—"Will Fox never know the importance of character?"

Fox was, in one sense, undoubtedly the greatest Englishman of his time. It may be doubted if there were ever a man more truly eloquent. He

was a statesman of broad views; he was humane
beyond his times, advocating the abolition of the
slave trade in opposition to his rival, Pitt.
Although spending all his life in politics when
political strife was bitter to the last degree, he
kept his sweetness of temper and had not a personal enemy. But in his private life he was dis-
solute, a gambler, a hard drinker, regardless of
all the obligations of morality. As a result, he
failed to secure the confidence of the country and
was subjected to the mortification of seeing himself continually outstripped by commonplace men,
by men immeasurably inferior, who had little
recommendation except their private virtues.

Not to mention other qualities, three component
parts in what is popularly called success are
energy, perseverance, and system. It is true that
either energy, perseverance, or system, may bring
a measure of success to its possessor. Many men
who have one quality well developed, suffer
because of their lack of training in the other two.
Napoleon had the three parts fully developed.
The result was a progressive, courageous, un-
flinching man. Never elsewhere was such a leader
so endowed and so weaponed; never has another
leader found such aids and followers. And what
was the result of this vast talent and power, of
these immense armies, burned cities, squandered
treasures, immolated millions of men, of this

demoralized Europe? He left France smaller, poorer, feebler than he found her. " When it was reported in Paris that the great Napoleon was dead," says a French writer, " I passed the Palais Royal, where a public crier called, ' Here's your account of the death of Bonaparte.' This cry which once would have appalled all Europe, fell perfectly flat. I entered," he adds, " several cafés, and found the same indifference—coldness everywhere; no one seemed interested or troubled. This man, who had conquered Europe and awed the world, had failed to keep the admiration of even his own countrymen. He had impressed the world with his marvellousness, and had inspired astonishment; but not love." Emerson says that " The Man of Destiny " did all that in him lay to live and thrive without moral principle. His was an experiment under the most favourable conditions, to test the powers of intellect without conscience. It was the nature of things, the eternal law of man and of the world, which balked and ruined him; and the result, in a million attempts of this kind, will be the same.

More than half a century ago there were gathered at Harvard University a company of students who loved the Republic and the example of its founders. One of these was Charles Sumner, whose noble career should be an inspiration to every political dreamer. Born, like Wendell Phillips, to wealth and historic fame, he, too, felt that his life should have a purpose, and both resolved to give their lives to the good of mankind. " In serving man," said Sumner, " there are nobler fields than those in which a Bayard ever conquered."

Massachusetts, quick to recognise in young Sumner a man whose inspiration was Duty, crowned him as her representative in her great struggle against wrong, and made him her voice of truth.

" Go to the doubtful members of the Legislature and use your influence," said his friends to him, when his election was pending. " Never," was Sumner's answer, " I will go to Cambridge, and no member of the Legislature shall see me until this contest is decided."

The Rhodians wrote the great Olympic ode of Pindar in letters of gold. The words of Charles Sumner in that supreme effort of his life, his speech called " Freedom National and Slavery Sectional," deserve a Rhodian inscription. " By no effort, by no desire of my own," he said, " I find myself a senator of the United States. Never before have I held public office of any kind. With the ample opportunities of private life I was content. No tombstone for me could bear a fairer inscription than this : ' Here lies one who, without honours or emoluments, did something for his fellowmen.' I forget myself and all personal consequences. The favor and goodwill of fellow-citizens, of my brethren in the senate, I am ready to sacrifice. All I am or can hope to be I give to this cause." Memorable in Massachusetts is that March day when, amid the tolling bells of Boston and the towns that surround Mount Auburn, amid the wail of trombones and the solemn music of Luther's "Judgment Hymn" in the dusk of a long, red twilight, Charles Sumner's body was lowered into the earth. He had found a field nobler than Bayard's. He had learned from life the simple truth, embodied in the last words upon his lips—"Character is everything."

Beecher says that we are all building a soul-house for eternity—yet with what differing architecture and what various care!

What if a man should see his neighbour getting workmen and building materials together, and should say to him, "What are you building?" and he should answer, "I don't exactly know. I am waiting to see what will come of it." And so walls are reared, and room is added to room, while the man looks idly on, and all the bystanders exclaim, "What a fool he is!" Yet this is the way many men are building their characters for eternity, adding room to room, without plan or aim, and thoughtlessly waiting to see what the effect will be.

We say that character is a product, but to what extent is it the product of outward circumstances, and to what extent the product of influences within? In brief, to what extent does the formation of character lie under the direct control of our own wills?

There is a great deal of discussion about the effect of environment upon character. That circumstances do, generally speaking, play a very important part in determining the bent of a child's character is not to be denied.

In our great museums you can see stone slabs with the marks of rain that fell ages upon ages before the first man appeared, and the footprint of some wild bird that passed across the beach in those olden times. The passing shower and the light foot left their prints on the soft sediment; then the centuries went by and the sediment hardened into stone; and there the prints remain, and will remain forever. So the child, so soft, so susceptible to all impressions, so joyous to receive new ideas, treasures them all up, gathers them all into itself, and retains them forever.

Robert Waters says that the face of a country has a strong influence on the disposition or temperament of its inhabitants. Dwellers in mountainous countries are generally of a cheerful, happy disposition; those of level, monotonous countries are strongly inclined to melancholy and pessimistic views. The people of the Alps, for instance, especially the peasants of the Tyrol, are celebrated for their lively disposition and their habit of constantly singing at their labour —in fact, Tyrolese songs are almost as famous as Scottish songs; while the Russians, inhabitants of the plain, are noted for their sad disposition, and their strong inclination toward melancholy views of life. Edmund Noble, in his interesting book on Russia, has this striking passage:

"The tendency universal in Russia is to pessimism. This penetrates all spheres of thought, gives its hues to every coterie and school, creates resemblances between the most diverse productions of the pen, restores as with a bond of gloom the shattered solidarity of society. Not to be pessimistic in Russia is to be divorced from all contact and sympathy with the national life; to be cut off, as if by foreign birth or by some monstrous denial of nature, from the tree of the national development. All influences and epochs have contributed to the tendency. A monotonous landscape, the loss of free institutions, Byzantinism with its cruel lawgiving and ascetic tyranny, the fiscal burden of the new state, the antitheses suggested by European culture, the crushing of the individual, the elimination from Russian life of all these healthy activities which engage citizenship in other countries, the harassing restrictions upon thought and movement, the state-created frivolities of society,—all these have contributed to the gloom of the mental atmosphere, until, to-day, pessimism may be said to be the normal condition of all Russian thought."

But the difference in the amount of mental

activity is the striking fact. Scotland, with her three and a half millions of inhabitants and thirty-one thousand square miles, has produced twenty times as many men of eminence in art and literature as Russia with her hundred million inhabitants and two millions of square miles. This, it may be said, is not because the one country is mountainous and picturesque, the other flat and dull, but because the one is free and the other enslaved. But what made the one free and the other enslaved? Is it not because mountain fastnesses inspire courage, create a spirit of independence, a defiance of danger, and a love of freedom? Is it not because a mountainous country breeds a strong, hardy race, sound in mind and limb, and noted for manly thinking and manly feeling? The mountaineer is accustomed from earliest youth to facing danger and difficulty, to looking upon dizzy precipices and overhanging rocks without fear, to encountering fierce storms and roaring torrents without flinching; while the inhabitant of the plain, living always on a level surface, where nothing hazardous is ever required of him, is seldom or never required to exert energy of body or mind, and remains an undeveloped creature.

So it is with the figurative plains and mountain regions of life. The conditions into which one is born predispose him to strength or weakness, but a lofty character does not require exalted circumstances for its development. A rich life may be lived amid poor surroundings.

" There are huge manufactories in this country," says Ian MacLaren, " with magnificent machinery, with chimneys belching forth clouds of black smoke to pollute the air, where they turn out carpets of most wonderful aspects, which would almost make you ill to look at, and which perish quickly in the using.

" Far away in the East in some poor little hut, an Eastern workman is working with threads of many colours beside him; he has been toiling for years, and, when he has finished, he will have turned out a single square of such beautiful colouring and such perfect workmanship that, when it comes to this country, it will be bought at a great price, and the owner's great-grandchildren will see it fresh and beautiful. So much for the great manufactory and the whirling wheels and the noise and the smoke; so much for the quietness and obscurity of a single workman! "

" How comest thou to smell so fragrantly? " asked the Persian poet Sadi of a clod of clay. " The sweetness is not in myself," replied the clay, " but I have been lying in contact with the rose." Yet the rose grew from that same clod of clay.

" When I found that I was black," said Alexandre Dumas, " I resolved to live as if I were white, and so force men to look below my skin."

" All the world cries, 'Where is the man who will save us?'" he says elsewhere. "'We want a man!' Don't look so far for this man. You have him at hand. This man—it is you, it is I, it is each one of us! . . . How to constitute one's self a man? Nothing harder, if one knows not how to will it; nothing easier, if one wills it."

" Though our character is formed by circumstances," says John Stuart Mill, " our own desires can do much to shape those circumstances; and what is really inspiriting and ennobling, in the doctrine of free-will, is the conviction that we have real power over the formation of our own character; our will, by influencing some of our circumstances, being able to modify our future habits or capacities of willing."

> Not in the clamour of the crowded street,
> Not in the shouts and plaudits of the throng,
> But in ourselves, are triumph and defeat.—
> LOWELL.

CHAPTER II

ONE'S VISION OF LIFE

EVERY really able man," says Emerson, " if you talk sincerely with him, considers his work, however much admired, as far short of what it should be. What is this better, this flying Ideal, but the perpetual promise of his Creator ? "

It is the glory and privilege of man that in the choice of his ideal he is free. An ideal of some kind he must have. It may be a heavenly vision leading toward the mountain top, or it may be an unworthy and degrading one that will drag him down to the depths. (" As a man thinketh in his heart, so is he.)

" If we would see the colour of our future," says Dean Farrar, " we must look for it in our present; if we would gaze on the star of our destiny, we must look for it in our hearts."

Did not John Milton, while yet a child, dream of writing an epic poem that the world would not willingly let die? The nebulous dream of the child became the fixed ideal of the youth. In his studies, his travels, through the stormy years of manhood, the vision never left him. Blind and old, the poet realised the dream of the child; and the heroic strains of " Paradise Lost " continue to echo through the centuries. " Still guides the heavenly vision," whispered the immortal poet, as he glided beyond the shadowy portals of life.

When Emerson counselled youth: " Hitch your wagon to a star," he did not mean that one is to place the ideal so high that it will be practically impossible to in anywise attain to it; but rather that it should be as a star, ever shining clear and bright to lead from height to height, from character to character. For, setting aside all thought of material progress, of success according to the general acceptation of the word, the first ideal should be that of a noble character, of constant growth toward that perfection urged upon us by the great Teacher, when He said, " Be ye therefore perfect, even as your Father which is in heaven is perfect." The ideal character will achieve true success in whatsoever calling the " soul's emphasis " has declared it shall follow. " Have ambition to be remembered," said Charles Sumner, " not as a great lawyer, doctor, merchant, scientist, manufacturer, or scholar, but as a great man, every inch a king." Our ideals, our longings, are the prophecies of our destinies.

There is always hope for the young man or

woman who has an affinity for the light; an up-ward aspiration like some trees, which have such an innate longing for the sunlight that they crowd past anything which impedes their progress, bending in their course around trees or any other obstruction, reaching up and up and up, until they get above the surrounding forest and bathe their proud heads in the bright free air.

A high ideal and a resolute determination to attain it are the moving factors of the world's progress. Without these we would have no great artists, poets, musicians, sculptors, inventors, or scientists. We would have no philanthropists, no noble men and women—Florence Nightingales, Livingstones, Maud Ballington Booths, or George Müllers—to devote their lives to the service of their fellow beings.

People with high ideals are the advance guard of humanity, the toilers who, with bent back and sweating brow, cut the smooth road over which man marches forward from generation to gene-ration.

The idealist is imaginative, hopeful, abounding with life and energy. He sees visions and dreams dreams, and lives in a world of hopeful, happy forces that continually radiate new energy—that generate it, indeed, and kindle the coals on the altar.

To him, at length, "strong and sure as the

Atlantic tides sweeping up the shore," comes inspiration with all its "hidings of power."

Bury a pebble, and it will obey the law of gravitation forever. Bury an acorn, and it will obey a higher law and grow. In the acorn is a vital force superior to the attraction of the earth. All plants and animals are climbing or reaching upward. Nature has whispered into the ear of all existence: "Look up." Man, above all, should have a celestial gravitation.

"It is not to taste sweet things, but to do noble and true things, and vindicate himself under God's heaven as a God-made man," says Carlyle, "that the poorest son of Adam dimly longs. Show him the way of doing that, and the dullest day-drudge kindles into a hero."

"Sad will be the day for any man," said Phillips Brooks, "when he becomes absolutely contented with the life he is living, with the thoughts he is thinking, and the deeds he is doing; when there is not forever beating at the doors of his soul some great desire to do something larger which he knows that he was meant and made to do, because he is a child of God. The ideal life," he adds, "the life of full completion, haunts us all; we feel the thing we ought to be beating beneath the thing we are."

"It seems to me we can never give up longing and wishing while we are thoroughly alive," says

George Eliot. " There are certain things we feel to be beautiful and good, and we must hunger after them."

" Man can never come up to his ideal standard," says Margaret Fuller Ossoli. " It is the nature of the immortal spirit to raise that standard higher and higher as it goes from strength to strength, still upward and onward."

This ideal is at once the source of inspiration without which progress in any direction is impossible, and the source of periods of profound discouragement. The only thing that is inexcusable and cowardly is to give up the struggle, to be content with dreaming noble things, as Kingsley says, instead of attempting to do them. Let us plan our soul houses in as lordly a way as we will, and having made our plans, deliberately set about bringing them to fulfillment by conduct consistent with our ideals.

We must not fall into the mistake of thinking that the ideal life can be realised only by those who do some great and commanding work in the world. The seamstress plying her needle from day to day to support existence, the poor cobbler at his bench, can as truly live the ideal life as the greatest benefactors of the race.

" It makes not so much difference where one stands," said Oliver Wendell Holmes, " as in what direction he is moving." It is the ideal you are striving after; not the work you are doing, but the spirit in which you do it, that will form the key-note of your life. You can live up to the best that is in you, no matter how humble your work or your station.

The question we should seriously ask ourselves at the outset is, What are our ideals? Toward what goal are our steps directed? It is a vulgar and degrading ambition which endeavours simply to secure a " respectable position in life."

God hides some ideal in every human soul. At some time in his life each feels a trembling, fear-ful longing to do some good thing. Life finds its noblest spring of excellence in this hidden impulse to do our best.

Perhaps the biggest word in America to-day, the word which fills our newspapers and maga-zines, and which excites social rivalry—a word which covers up crime and is an excuse every-where for misdemeanour, the word which the American child is taught to lisp with reverence and worship almost from the cradle, the " be all and end all " of many a human life, the word which covers a multitude of sins— is " success." Many an American youth's model is the poor boy who can go to Chicago, or New York, or Boston, without a penny, and die a millionaire. This to him is success; and why shouldn't it be? He sees the whole world running after the millionaire, regardless of who he is or how he got his money. No matter how he made it, spent it, or left it; few will ask whether he was rich in intellect, broad, beautiful, and noble in his life, or narrow, mean, avaricious, and grasping—if he left a million, he was called successful. No matter if he ground the very life out of his employees; no matter if others grew poorer that he might become rich; no matter if he poisoned and lessened the value of every acre of land in his neighbourhood; no matter if his children were mentally and morally starved and his home wretched; if he left a million, it was said that he had triumphed. This is the philosophy of the street which the boy breathes in as he learns to talk.

Don't teach the young that " success " in acquiring wealth or position is the only condition of happiness.

Millions of bright boys and girls are destined to spend their lives in the constant service of others —in helping the sick, the poor, the unfortunate, the helpless—and practically they will never have an opportunity to become either well educated or very rich. But they must not expect to be forever miserable unless they succeed according to the popular standard of success. Many a poor woman, who spends her life in the sick room or in menial service, has reached a success infinitely higher than has many a millionaire.

Do not strive to reach impossible goals. It is wholly in your power to develop yourself, but not necessarily to make yourself a king. Too many are deluded by ambition beyond the power of attainment, or tortured by aspirations totally disproportionate to their capacity for execution. You may, indeed, confidently hope to become eminent in usefulness and power, but only as you build upon a broad foundation of self-culture.

The young man or woman who starts out in life with an ideal of success limited to the accumulation of wealth, or the performance of some deed that men will applaud, is to be pitied, for measured by such a standard the great majority of people are failures.

Happy the boy or girl who has the inestimable advantage of living close to a noble character, a parent, friend, or teacher, who will not only be a worthy model to imitate, but will constantly hold before the growing mind high ideals, will introduce it to the literature that uplifts, inspire it with a passion for excellence. The influence of parents and teachers in guiding youth toward exalted ideas is inestimable.

For good or for ill, how great is the power of friendship, of associations, of example! It is true that our associates are often chosen for us by circumstances; we should be the more careful, then, of the choices that lie within our power.

It was said of Dugald Stewart that he breathed the love of virtue into whole generations of pupils. "To me," says the late Lord Cockburn, "his lectures were like the opening of the heavens. I felt that I had a soul. His noble views, unfolded in glorious sentences, elevated me into a higher world. . . . They changed my whole nature."

It is not possible for every schoolboy to select his schoolmaster; but it is within the power of every living soul to choose whom he will for a master in the school of life.

One's ideal, or life-pattern, is the line which bounds his vision; and, as long as this ideal, or pattern, remains unchanged, the mind and life of the entire man must remain unchanged also. Elizabeth Stuart Phelps speaks, in "The Story of Avis," of one who had "a high ideal in cup cakes," which will remind those who knew her of a woman to whom beautiful "hooked" and braided rugs furnished her highest ideal. She did her housework, and every hour which could be spared was devoted to producing, in all the colours of the rainbow, animals and birds of every conceivable or, rather, inconceivable kind, on these rug canvases. She had "no time" for reading or for joining her husband or children in their recreations or games, or to keep in touch with any of the great movements of the age. Her life was, like her ideal, comparatively insignificant, narrow, devoid of the example it should have been to her children, the companionship it should have held for her husband, and the development it should have had for herself.

Without high ideals, we are like the eagle whose wings have been clipped. We were meant to soar, and our ideals are the wings on which we mount "toward the vaulted skies." Without them we hover near the earth. Dr. Collyer says that Darwin's suggestion as to the evolution of the eagle's wings is an instructive one. The desire to ascend was there before the wings, and through countless ages of development the processes of formation and adaptation went on, until at length, with mighty pinions, seven feet from tip to tip, the eagle soared aloft toward the sun. Of us it may be said that every well-meant trial and intention is part of a great process; each starts some feather in the eagle's wing.

The noblest character would soon degenerate, if it should lose the love of excellence. This is the mainspring of all great character. This passion for excellence is the voice of God, bidding us up and on, lest we forget our divine origin and degenerate to barbarism again. This principle is the guardian of the human race. It is God's voice in man; it is the still small voice that whispers "right" or "wrong" to every act. What is the ideal we have of our own lives, but the gift of the Creator, when he fashioned us in his own image?

"Conditions favourable or unfavourable to good character may be inherited," says Rev. George A. Gordon, " but the thing itself, good character, cannot be inherited. It is a product, a beautiful fabric woven upon the loom of personal activity, constructed out of aspirations and prayers, visions of the ideal, high resolves, dreams of a juster rela- tion to man and a happier communion with God; it is these turned into solid reality and shining like cloth of gold through the continuous effort of the faithful and successful will."

It is within the province of your will to decide once for all whether you will pattern your life after perfect or imperfect models. If you decide wisely, and persist in your choice, you will grow unto the stature of a noble manhood or woman- hood.

CHAPTER III

SELF-HONOR

THE first step to failure is the first doubt of yourself."

A child should be taught to accept a successful life, to believe that he is born to develop the divine gifts bestowed upon him, as the acorn is destined to become an oak. He should grow up in this firm belief. Teachers often lessen their pupils' faith in themselves by telling them they are going to fail in their recitations or examinations, instead of inspiring them with hope and confidence.

It would, in thousands of cases, do away with years of uncertain groping, doubt, and fear, if children were, from their first days of understanding, made to feel that their parents and teachers respect their ideas and abilities, and expect important future work from them. A person on whom another relies, and in whom he believes, is a thousand times more likely to be reliable and worthy of belief than the one from whom nothing is expected. This fact was continually and conclusively proved by that prince of instructors, Thomas Arnold of Rugby, who kept thousands of boys from disgraceful escapades because they "couldn't disappoint the old man," who believed in them as scholars and as gentlemen.

If we would succeed, we must expect success, and not create an unfavourable atmosphere and environment by constant distrust of ourselves and expressions of doubt. The fear of failure, and constant contemplation of its possibilities, have kept many a noble soul from succeeding. (Believe firmly that, if you do not find a way, you can make one, and you will triumph.)

When an intelligent, forceful person voices a conviction of what he can and will do, it is the part of wisdom to give heed and credence to the word thus uttered, though no past acts stand sponsor for them.

"Why, sir," said John C. Calhoun in Yale College, when a fellow student ridiculed his intense application to study, "I am forced to make the most of my time, that I may acquit myself creditably when in Congress." A laugh greeted this speech, when he exclaimed, "Do you doubt it? I assure you if I were not convinced of my ability to reach the national capital as a representative within the next three years, I would leave college this very day."

What seems to us disagreeable egotism in

others is often but a strong expression of confidence in their ability to attain. Great men have usually had great confidence in themselves. Wordsworth felt sure of his place in the history of English literature, and never hesitated to say so. Dante predicted his own fame. Kepler said it did not matter whether his contemporaries read his books or not: " I may well wait a century for a reader, since God has waited for thousands of years for an observer like myself." " Fear not," said Julius Cæsar to his pilot frightened in a storm, " thou bearest Cæsar and his good fortune."

Froude wrote: " A tree must be rooted in the soil before it can bear flowers or fruit. A man must learn to stand upright on his own feet, to respect himself, to be independent of charity or accident. It is on this basis only that any superstructure of intellectual cultivation worth having can possibly be built."

Elias Howe was ridiculed for neglecting his family and work, and living in poverty and wretchedness while experimenting on the sewing machine, but he had the utmost confidence in its final triumph, and, as a result, lived to give the world one of the most useful implements of labour.

The list of those who have, amid unbelief, jeers, discouragements, banked, so to speak, solely upon their belief in themselves when no one else would give them credit, is long. It includes Samuel F. B. Morse and Cyrus W. Field, and runs back to Columbus and beyond him to many an ancient name well known to this day throughout the world.

For one who cannot thoroughly respect himself, the high and abiding confidence of others is impossible.

We are all familiar with people who are constantly depreciating themselves, decrying their hard luck, and complaining that fate is against them. How can a man expect to succeed when he has lost faith in his own powers? A hypnotist can so deprive his subject of confidence in his strength that he cannot rise from his chair, even if he be an athlete. People who go through life bemoaning their luck, and thinking that success is for others, but not for them, must expect failure, for self-confidence is the very foundation of all accomplishment.

("Well-matured and well-disciplined talent is always sure of a market," said Washington Irving; "but it must not cower at home and expect to be sought for.") — *Advertise.*

The world believes in the man who believes in himself, but it has little use for the timid, for one never certain of himself, who cannot rely on his own judgment, who craves advice from others, and is afraid to go ahead on his own account.

There is little room, in this crowding, competing age, for the timid, vacillating youth. He who would succeed, to-day, must not only be brave, but must also dare to take chances. He who waits for certainty never wins.

It is the man with a positive nature, who feels that he is equal to the emergency and who believes he can do the thing he attempts, who wins the confidence of his fellow man. He is beloved because he is brave and self-sufficient.

Those who have accomplished great things in the world have been, as a rule, bold, aggressive, and self-confident. They dared to step out from the crowd and act in an original way. They were not afraid to be generals. They took the high counsel which Emerson gave when he said: " Insist on yourself; never imitate. Your own gift you can present every moment with the cumulative force of a whole life's cultivation; but of the adopted talent of another you have only an extemporaneous half-possession. (That which each can do best, none but his Maker can teach him.") *Rely in Him.*

There is everything in assuming the part or character you desire to play in life's drama. If you are to take the part of a successful man, you must assume the mental attitude, the outward mien, of a successful person—must put yourself, as it were, in his place.

A keen observer can pick out upon the street the man who has failed in life. There is no decision in his step, his uncertain gait indicates lack of confidence in himself; his dress, his bearing, everything points toward incompetence. His shiftlessness is pictured in every movement of his body.

On the other hand, it is easy to pick out the successful, the man of force, by the way he carries himself. If he is a leader, every step, every movement indicates it; there is assurance in his bearing, he walks as if he were master of himself, as if he believed in his ability to do things, to bring about results. His self-confident air is an index of the success, the mastery, he has attained.

The world has a right to look to us for our own rating. We stamp our own value upon ourselves and cannot expect to pass for more.

Are you introduced into society? People will look into your face and eye, to see what estimate you place upon yourself. If they see a low mark, why should they trouble themselves to investigate to see if you have not rated yourself too low? They know you have lived with yourself a good while and ought to know your own value better than they.

" My success has always turned upon one

maxim," said Nathan Rothschild to Thomas Buxton. "I said, 'I can do what another man can,' and so I am a match for all the rest of them."

If you would succeed up to the limit of your possibilities, hold constantly to the belief that you are success-organised, and that you will succeed, no matter what opposes. (Never allow a shadow of doubt to enter your mind that the Creator intended you to win in life's battle.) *But dont get a swelled head.*

It is wonderful what power self-confidence has to marshal all the faculties and unite their strength. No matter how many talents a man may possess—if he be lacking in self-confidence he can never use them to the best advantage; he cannot unify mental action and so harmonise his powers as to bring them to bear effectively upon any one point.

More men fail through ignorance of their strength than through knowledge of their weakness.

In order to succeed in life, it is just as necessary to have self-trust as to have ability; and, if you do not possess the former, one of the best means of acquiring it is to assume that you already have whatever ability you need for life's affairs. Carry yourself with a self-confident air, and you will not only inspire others with a belief in your strength, but you will come to believe in it yourself.

Believe in yourself. You may succeed when

others do not believe in you, but never when you do not believe in yourself.

"The pious and just honouring of ourselves," it was said by Milton, "may be thought the fountain-head from whence every laudable and worthy enterprise issues forth."

CHAPTER IV

GETTING THE WHIP HAND OF YOURSELF

THE secret of all success," says Mrs. Oliphant, " is to know how to deny yourself. If you once learn to get the whip hand of yourself, that is the best educator. (Prove to me that you can control yourself, and I'll say you're an educated man, and without this all education is good for next to nothing.")

In early life Abraham Lincoln was exceedingly quick-tempered and combative. He learned self-control later, and became one of the most patient of men. He said of this trait: " I learned during the Black Hawk War the necessity of controlling my temper, and that good habit has stuck by me ever since." It was one of the chief elements that made possible his wonderful control of others.

General Grant was equally calm, self-reliant, and unperturbed, either at the sight of regiments breaking in defeat, or before the hero-worship of a nation upon the return of his victorious army into Washington in the grand review of the Army of the Republic.

" It is the man that is cool and collected,"

remarks Diderot, the French philosopher, " that is master of his countenance, his voice, his actions, his gestures, of every part, who can work upon others at his pleasure." " No one who cannot master himself," says Goethe, " is worthy to rule, and only he can rule."

Take the case of Charles Stewart Parnell, the great Irish leader. His temper as a young man seemed uncontrollable. He was expelled from Cambridge because he knocked down two men, one of whom, seeing him sitting at the side of a road, said: " Hullo, what's the matter with this 'ere cove? " His own lawyer admitted Parnell's fault, and the foolish display of his prowess cost him twenty-five guineas at the hands of a jury.

Not only anger, but embarrassment, over-powered him. In attempting to make his first speech, he almost fainted on the rostrum, and the discouraged voters elected another man.

Years afterwards, Mr. Gladstone, in speaking of Parnell when he held the balance of power in the British Empire, said:

" Parnell was the most remarkable man I ever met. I drew up (in a speech) a rather strong indictment against him. Well, he sat still all the time, and was quite immovable. He listened attentively, courteously, but showed no feeling, no excitement, no concern. The immobility of the man, the laconic way of dealing with the subject, his utter indifference to the opinion of the House—the whole thing was extraordinary and unlike what one was accustomed to under such circumstances!"

Among the minor virtues, probably the habit of self-control in speech holds the most important place in the life of a woman. The acquirement of this habit must begin early or it will never be attained save with great difficulty. It must be formed in girlhood if not well begun in childhood. I have seen the happiness of many a fair life ruined by the want of power to suppress the word of bitterness, contempt, or anger, under what might be called " reasonable provocation." There are times when one's only duty is to keep from talking.

Mme. de Maintenon declared that the height of power in women, so far as manners are concerned, rests in tranquillity. Half the troubles of life would be saved, if people would remember that silence is golden when they are vexed or annoyed.

Charles Buxton declared that a man or a woman may be by nature highly irritable, and yet be sweet, tender, gentle, loving, sociable, kind, charitable, thoughtful for others, unselfish, and generous.

To remain calm and unmoved under severe provocation, to resist every irritable impulse, every inclination to say harsh, unkind things, even when one's most vulnerable point has been assailed, requires spiritual stamina and force of character far greater than that demanded of the hero in a merely physical contest.

Some people are weak enough to think that a quick, ungovernable temper is an indication of a lofty spirit. This is the very opposite of the truth. As a rule, a fiery temper, or, rather, the giving way to it, shows a lack of mental balance. Truly great characters are nearly always serene and not easily moved from their balance.

"Strength of character," says F. W. Robertson, "consists of two things—power of will and power of self-restraint. It requires two things, therefore, for its existence—strong feelings and strong command over them. Now it is here we make a grand mistake—we mistake strong feelings for strong character. The man who bears all before him, before whose frown domestics tremble, and whose bursts of fury make the children of his household quake—because he has his will obeyed and his own way in all things— him we call a strong man. The truth is, he is a weak man. It is his passions that are strong; he that is mastered by them is weak. You must measure a man by the strength of the feelings he subdues, not by the power of those which subdue him. And hence composure is very often the highest result of strength. Did we ever see a man receive a flagrant insult, and only grow a little pale, and then reply quietly? That is a man spiritually strong. Or did we ever see a man in anguish stand as if carved out of solid rock, mastering himself? Or one that, bearing a hopeless daily trial, remains silent, and never tells the world what cankers his home peace? That is strength. He who, with strong passions, remains chaste; he who, keenly sensitive, with many powers of indignation in him, can be provoked and yet restrain himself and forgive— these are the strong men, the spiritual heroes."

There is nothing finer in the world than " The Kingship of Self-Control." " Man," says William George Jordan, " has two creators—his God and himself. His first creator furnishes him the raw material of his life, and the laws in conformity with which he can make that life what he will. His second creator—himself—has marvellous powers, which he rarely realises. *It is what a man makes of himself that counts.* Man in his weakness is the creature of circumstances; man in his strength is the creator of circumstances. Whether he be victim or victor depends largely on himself. The self-control that is seen in the most spectacular instances in history, and in the simplest phases of daily life, is precisely the same in kind and quality, differing only in degree. This control man can attain if he will; it is but a matter of paying the price. The power of self-control is one of the great qualities that differentiates man from the lower animals. He is the only animal capable of a moral struggle or a moral conquest. Every step in the progress of the world has been a new control. It has been escaping from the tyranny of a fact to the understanding and mastery of that fact."

" At each moment of man's life he is either a king or a slave. As he surrenders to a wrong appetite, to any human weakness, as he falls prostrate in hopeless subjection to any condition, to any environment, to any failure, he is a slave. *As he day by day crushes out human weakness, masters opposing elements within him,* and day by day re-creates a new self from the sin and folly of his past—he is a king."

Self-control is of fundamental importance in the formation and development of character and it intimately concerns success in life.

Every human being is conscious of two natures. One is ever reaching up after the good, the true, and the noble—is aspiring after all that uplifts, elevates, and purifies. It is the God-side of man, the image of the Creator, the immortal side, the spiritual side. It is the gravitation of the soul faculties toward their Maker. The other is the bestial side, which gravitates downward.

The individual can attain self-control in great things only through self-control in little things. He must study himself to discover what is the weak point in his armour, what is the element in him that keeps him from his fullest success. This is the characteristic upon which he should begin his exercise in self-control. Is it selfishness, vanity, cowardice, morbidness, temper, laziness, worry, mind-wandering, lack of purpose?—Whatever form human weakness assumes in the masquerade of life, he must discover. He must then live each day as if his whole existence was telescoped down to the single day before him.

With no idle regret for the past, no useless worry for the future, he should live that day as if it were his only day—the only day left for him to assert all that is best in him, the only day left for him to conquer all that is worst in him. He should master the weak element within him at each slight manifestation from moment to moment. Each moment then must be a victory for it or for him. Will he be a king or a slave?

Learn to act nobly and grandly on every occasion that presents itself. Every occasion should be a great occasion. If you shirk duty or compromise manhood, your character is weakened. Must I acknowledge myself inferior to circumstances, and succumb to petty annoyances and little miseries? Mind is superior to matter; and wings of hope, of aspiration, of expectation, of confidence, were given us to lift ourselves above the petty storms of life, which rage about inferior beings and make miserable those who are power-less to mount above them.

CHAPTER V

OUR RECORDING ANGEL

ALL our deeds are recorded with an iron pen even to the smallest detail. The Recording Angel is no myth—it is found in ourselves, it is the law of habit.

Habit has been sometimes called our second mother, and a good mother. There is a tendency in the nervous system to repeat the same mode of action at regularly recurring intervals. Dr. Combe says that all nervous diseases have a marked tendency to observe regular periods. " If we repeat any kind of mental effort at the same hour daily, we at length find ourselves entering upon it without premeditation when the time approaches."

This pertains to the nervous system in all animal life. It is illustrated in fire-engine horses, as related by Dr. Vance. " In Nashville," says the Doctor, " the fire department has an engine located on the eastern side of the Cumberland River. To reach the city hall from this engine-house it is necessary to go six blocks west, down Woodland Street, cross the long bridge which spans the Cumberland, and turn into the public square.

At the first alarm of fire, it is the duty of the crew of the East Nashville engine to go immediately to the city hall and wait there as a reserve. At a second alarm, they go into action. One night the alarm sounded. Quickly the horses took their places, the fireman occupying his position in the rear of the engine; but, as the horses dashed out at full gallop, the driver missed his step and was left behind. Down the street the team raced at full speed, the fireman in the rear blissfully ignorant that no hands were on the reins. Across the long bridge, around the curve, and to their appointed place in front of the city hall the horses galloped, and there they stopped, to await farther orders. As the belated driver rushed up breathless, to find all was well, he realised that trunk lines of habit can be laid in the body of a horse as well as in that of a man. Resting his cheek against the faces of his dumb friends, he praised them and patted them, and was proud to be the driver of such a team."

It is possible for a human being thus to make habit the friend of duty.

" The great thing in all education is to make our nervous system our ally instead of our enemy. It is to fund and capitalise our acquisition, and live at ease upon the interest of the fund. For this we must make automatic and habitual, as soon as possible, as many useful actions as we can, and guard against growing into ways that are likely to be disadvantageous to us, as we would guard against the plague."

Deep in the very nature of animate existence is this principle of facility and inclination, acquired by repetition, which we call habit.

A man's entire life is spent writing his own biography. Beyond his control is the phonograph of the soul, which registers faithfully every thought, however feeble, every act, however small, every sensation, however slight, every impulse, every motive, every aspiration, every ambition, every effort, every stimulus, on the cerebral tissue.

If a young man neglects his mind and heart,— if he indulges himself in vicious courses and forms habits of inefficiency and slothfulness—he experiences a loss which no subsequent effort can retrieve.

Habit is practically, for a middle-aged person, fate; for is it not practically certain that what I have done for twenty years, I shall repeat to-day? What are the chances for a man who has been lazy and indolent all his life starting to-morrow morning to be industrious; or if a spendthrift, frugal; if a libertine, virtuous; if a profane and foul-mouthed man, clean and chaste?

"Habit a second nature? Habit is ten times nature," exclaimed the Duke of Wellington.

" Where the habits have been judiciously formed in the first instance," says Dr. Carpenter, " the tendency is an extremely useful one, prompting us to do that spontaneously which might otherwise require a powerful effort of the will. The author can speak from long and varied experience of the immense saving of exertion which arises from the formation of methodical habits of mental labor."

Any occupation is easiest to him who has familiarised himself with its processes by repeated practice, and he who has become familiar with those processes is most likely to succeed. As men acquire greater and greater skill in the various trades or professions, it becomes more and more difficult for one to do many kinds of work in a satisfactory manner, in competition with others. Jacks-of-all-trades are gradually becoming scarcer as we advance in civilisation. We must concentrate our energies upon definite purposes if we wish to excel. " I have but one lamp by which my feet are guided," said Patrick Henry, " and that is the lamp of experience."

" Mysterious and unrecorded influences extending over untold generations have combined to make every man what he is, and to endow him with a personality which he can never escape from, nor transcend. The boy, the man, can no more run away from his parents than he can from himself. He may renounce and cast out the traits which he has inherited, but he cannot get rid of them; unbidden and unnoticed, they will slink back and abide with him forever; they are not his servants, but belong to his family, his clan, his race."

"You reap what you sow—not something else, but that," said F. W. Robertson; "an act of love makes the soul more loving, a deed of humbleness deepens humbleness. The thing reaped is the very thing sown, multiplied a hundredfold. You have sown the seed of life; you reap life everlasting."

"In all the wide range of accepted British maxims," said Thomas Hughes, "there is none, take it all in all, more thoroughly abominable than the one as to the sowing of wild oats. Look at it on what side you will, and I defy you to make anything but a devil's maxim of it. What a man, be he young, old, or middle-aged, sows, that, and nothing else, shall he reap. The only thing to do with wild oats is to put them carefully into the hottest part of the fire, and get them burnt to dust, every seed of them. If you sow them, no matter in what ground, up they will come with long, tough roots and luxuriant stalks and leaves, as sure as there is a sun in heaven. The devil, too, whose special crop they are, will see that they thrive; and you, and nobody else, will have to reap them."

It is related of Plato that he reproved a boy for playing at some foolish game. " Thou reprovest me," said the boy, " for a very little thing." " But custom," replied Plato, " is not a little thing." The whole secret of character is bound up in that one word, custom. Bad custom, consolidated into habit, is such a tyrant that men sometimes cling to vices even while they curse them. They have become the slaves of habits whose power they are impotent to resist. Hence Locke has said that to create and maintain that vigour of mind which is able to contest the empire of habit may be regarded as one of the chief ends of moral discipline.

" There is no fault or folly of my life," said Ruskin, " that does not rise against me and take away my joy, and shorten my power of possession, of sight, of understanding; and every past effort of my life, every gleam of righteousness or good in it, is with me now to help me in my grasp of this hour and its vision."

" My character to-day is, for the most part, simply the resultant of all the thoughts I have ever had, of all the feelings I have ever cherished, and all the deeds I have ever performed," says the Rev. C. H. Parkhurst. " It is the entirety of my previous years packed and crystalised into the present moment. So that character is the quintessence of biography; so that everybody who knows my character—and there is no keeping character under cover—knows what for forty or more years I have been doing and thinking. Character is, for the most part, simply habit become fixed."

Rectitude is only the confirmed habit of doing what is right. Some men cannot tell a lie; the habit of truth telling is fixed, it has become incorporated with their nature. Their characters bear the indelible stamp of veracity. You and I know men whose slightest word is unimpeachable; nothing could shake our confidence in them. There are other men who cannot speak the truth; their habitual insincerity has made a twist in their characters, and this twist appears in their speech.

As our growth is by littles, so is our decay. When a wind storm sweeps over the forest, it is the weakened trees that fall. We are not often overthrown by a sudden wind of trial unless we have weakened our souls by habitual yielding to the power of evil in a thousand small temptations. Nor do we overcome in one great effort, but in a constant endeavour, lasting through the years of life.

" Habit is a cable," says an old motto. " We weave a thread of it each day; by and by it will become so strong that we cannot break it."

After a man's habits are well set, about all he can do is to sit by and observe which way he is going. Regret it as he may, how helpless is a weak man bound by the mighty cable of habit, twisted from the tiny threads of single acts which he thought were absolutely within his control.

The events which go to form the character, it is said, accumulate constantly to the end of life, determined by the choice that was made at first, like the accumulating waters of the river as it rolls on, augmenting its volume and its velocity, until life is lost in the broad ocean of eternity.

Drop a stone down a precipice. By the law of gravitation it sinks with rapidly increasing momentum. If it falls sixteen feet the first second, it will fall forty-eight feet the next second, and eighty feet the third second, and one hundred and forty-four feet the fifth second; and, if it falls for ten seconds, it will in the last second rush through three hundred and four feet. Habit is cumulative. After each act of your life, you are not the same person as before, but quite another, better or worse, but not the same. There has been something added to, or deducted from your weight of character.

A community may be surprised and shocked at some crime. The man was seen on the street yesterday, or in his store, but he showed no indication that he would commit such a crime to-day.

Yet the crime committed to-day is but a regular and natural sequence of what the man did yesterday and the day before. It is the momentum made up from a thousand deviations from the truth and right, for there is a great difference between going just right and a little wrong. It is the result of that mysterious power which the repeated act has of getting itself repeated again and again.

Experience shows that, quicker than almost any other physical agency, alcohol breaks down a man's power of self-control. But the physical evils of intemperance, great as they are, are slight, compared with the moral injury it produces. It is not simply that vices and crimes almost inevitably follow the loss of rational self-direction, which is the invariable accompaniment of intoxication; manhood is lowered and finally lost by the sensual tyranny of appetite. The drunken man has given up the reins of his nature to a fool or a fiend, and he is driven fast to base or unutterably foolish ends.

"In the conduct of life," says a French writer, "habits count for more than maxims, because habit is a living maxim and becomes flesh and instinct. To reform one's maxims is nothing; it is but to change the title of a book. To learn new habits is everything, for it is to reach the substance of life."

" On the acquisition of a new habit, or in leaving off an old one," says Professor James, " we must take care to launch ourselves with as strong and decided an initiative as possible. Accumulate all the possible circumstances which shall reinforce the right motives; put yourself assiduously in conditions that encourage the new way; make engagements incompatible with the old; take a public pledge, if the case allows; in short, envelop your resolution with every aid you know. This will give your new beginning such a momentum that the temptation to break down will not occur as soon as it might; and every day during which a breakdown is postponed adds to the chances that it will not occur at all.

" The second maxim is: Never suffer an exception to occur till the new habit is securely rooted in your life. Each lapse is like letting fall a ball of string which one is carefully winding up; a single slip undoes more than a great many turns will wind again."

" Refrain to-night," says Shakespeare, " and that shall lend a hand of easiness to the next abstinence; the next more easy; for use can almost change the stamp of nature, and either curb the devil, or throw him out with wondrous potency."

When the late John Sherman was secretary of state, a young man, the son of one of Sherman's schoolmates, wrote to him for assistance. He said that he had fallen so low in life that there was no place for him but the gutter; that existence had become a burden, and that he wanted to die. To-day, this same young man is a prosperous merchant in New York City. He says that his position is due to the advice given him by John Sherman, in answer to his letter.

He gave permission to publish the letter, which the owner guards more carefully than all his other possessions. Mr. Sherman wrote:

"You say that your life has been a failure, and that you are thirty years old, and ready to die. You say that you cannot find work, and that you see no hope in life. You say that your friends do not care to speak to you now. Let me tell you that you have reached that point in life when a man must see the very best prospects for his future career. You, at thirty, stand on the bridge that divides youth and manhood. Unless you are physically deformed, go to work at any honest work, if it only brings you a dollar a day. Then learn to live within that dollar. Pay no more than ten cents for a meal, and twenty cents for a bed, and save as much of the balance as you can, and with the same intensity as you would save your mother's life. Make the most of your appearance. Do not dress gaudily, but cleanly. Abandon liquor as you would abandon a pestilence, for liquor is the curse that wrecks more lives than all the horrors of the world combined. If you are a man of brains, as your letter leads me to believe you are, wait until you are in a condition to seek your level, and then seek it with courage and tenacity. It may take time to reach it; it may take years, but you will surely reach it—you will turn from the workingman into the business man, or the professional man, with so much ease that you will marvel at it. But have one ideal, and aim for it. No ship ever reached its port by sailing for a dozen other ports at the same time. Be contented, for without contentment there is no love or friendship, and without those blessings life is a hopeless case. Learn to love your books, for there is pleasure, instruction, and friendship in books. Go to church, for the church helps to ease the pains of life. But never be a hypocrite; if you cannot believe in God, believe in your honour. Listen to music whenever you can, for music charms the mind, and fills a man with lofty ideals. Cheer up! Never want to die. Why, I am twice your age, and over, and I do not want to die. Get out into the world. Work, eat, sleep, read, and talk about the great events of the day, even if you are forced to go among labourers. Take the first honest work you get, and then be steady, patient, industrious, saving, kind, polite, studious, temperate, ambitious, gentle, loving, strong, honest, courageous, and contented. Be all these, and, when thirty years more have passed away, just notice how young and beautiful the world is, and how young and happy you are!"

The Law of Habit touches upon everything we do in life. "Regular work," says a recent writer, "and equally regular recreation, daily work and daily recreation, those make up a wholesome regimen.

"Kant of Königsberg, laboured on year after year, without haste and without rest, working all the day and half the night, except that every afternoon he appeared at precisely the same hour in his garden for a long walk under the linden trees; Heine says that the neighbours used to set their watches by him, little thinking of the philosophical systems that the brown-coated old professor was calmly destroying each morning to make room for his own.

"John Ericsson was an example of the efficacy of regular habits; he lived for twenty years in one house in New York, eating almost exactly the same kind of breakfast and dinner every day for twenty years, and spending nearly all his time at his desk; he lived on graham bread, fruit, tea, chops, and steak; he took an hour's walk every evening; he worked at desk or drafting-board all the rest of the time from six in the morning till midnight.

" Perhaps more remarkable than either Kant or Ericsson as a steady machine was the great French dictionary-maker, Émile Littré. His book, which consumed thirteen years in the mere printing (1859-1872), is one of the three or four really monumental lexicons. He did not begin the task till he was forty-five, and he laboured at it incessantly for thirty years. He has himself told the method of his daily work. The wonder is that he remained cheerful and charming throughout the whole period. He says :

" My rule of life included the twenty-four hours of the day and night, so as to bestow the least possible amount of time on the current calls of existence. . . . I rose at eight ; very late, you will say, for so busy a man. Wait an instant. Whilst they put my bedroom in order, which was also my study, I went downstairs with some work in hand. It was thus, for example, that I composed the preface of the Dictionary. I had learned from Chancellor d'Agnesseau the value of unoccupied minutes. At nine I set to work to correct proofs until the hour of our midday meal. At one I resumed work, and wrote my papers for the ' Journal des Savants,' to which I was from 1855 a regular contributor. From three to six I went on with the dictionary. At six, punctually, we dined, which took about an hour. They say it is unwholesome to work directly after dinner, but I have never found it so. It is so much time won from the exigencies of the body. Starting again at seven in the evening, I stuck to the dictionary. My first stage took me to midnight, when my wife and daughter (who were my assistants) retired. I then worked on till three in the morning, by which time my daily task was usually completed. If it was not, I worked on later; and, more than once, in the long days of summer, I have put out my lamp and continued to work by the light of the coming dawn. However, at three in the morning, I generally laid down my pen and put my papers in order for the following day—that day which had already begun. Habit and regularity had extinguished all excitement in my work. I fell asleep as easily as a man of leisure does, and woke at eight, as men of leisure do. But these vigils were not without their charm. A nightingale had built her nest in a row of limes that crosses the garden, and she filled the silence of the night and of the country with her limpid and tuneful notes.' "

" Physiologists tell us," says Robert Waters, " that it takes twenty-eight years for the brain to attain its full development. If this is so, why should not one be able, by his own efforts, to give this long-growing organ a particular bent, a peculiar character? Why should the will not be brought to bear upon the formation of the brain as well as of the backbone?" The will is merely our steam power, and we may put it to any work we please. It will do our bidding, whether it be building up character, or tearing it down. It may be applied to building up a habit of truthfulness and honesty, or of falsehood and dishonour. It will help build up a man or a brute, a hero or a coward. It will brace up resolution until one may almost perform miracles or it may be dissipated in irresolution and inaction until life is a wreck. It will hold you to your task until you have formed a powerful habit of industry and application, until idleness and inaction are painful, or it will lead you into indolence and listlessness until every effort will be disagreeable and success impossible."

A wise teacher says to his pupils: "What we are this minute, what we do this minute, what we think this minute, will be read in our future characters, as truly as a word spoken into a phonograph will be reproduced in the future."

A writer upon indoor games and outdoor sports, insists that "The foundation of all the qualities of a man are laid in a great measure in the games and plays of childhood, and their nature determines whether the result will be good or evil. It is very necessary that the greatest care should be exercised at this time of a boy's life, in supervising his recreations and amusements. He should learn that subordination of self and co-operation are essentials of successful team work. He finds that, if he has no consideration for others, he will receive little himself. Self-control, honesty, and other moral qualities can be made habits or not as the boy observes them in play. The reason for this is that play is real to the young child. It is his serious business. It is more true to him than the affairs of grown people, and therefore it is necessary that false ideals should get no chance to be adopted; for, as the child grows older, he does not discard the old and then get a new set of ideas, but to what he first learned he adds the experience of his age, whatever that may be. It is the first knowledge that makes the point of view from which all later ideas and events are considered, and which modifies them."

What is true of education by games is true of education in manners—it is of the utmost importance to start right.

Some people find it impossible to keep still for a moment. They must have hands or feet or some part of the body in continual motion. I have known boys and girls to play with their knives and forks and drum with their fingers on the table. To sit quietly in repose seems to be a lost art with them. Chewing gum, holding toothpicks or other bits of wood between the teeth, playing with the under lip, or constantly rocking, are all harmless but disagreeable.

While habits of this class do not mar the character or lower the morals, they detract from that perfect good breeding which is no small factor in gaining success, as they annoy fastidious employers, repel hostesses, and are often trials even to one's friends. They should be done away with just as surely as more harmful habits.

This same law holds good in repetitions of acts of all kinds, whether moral or immoral. The habit of rising at a certain hour in the morning, of meeting engagements promptly, of being always courteous, of being methodical and systematic, of stating everything exactly, of being scrupulously honest, of being never idle, would be a blessing in after life which could hardly be overestimated. These habits would wear their beaten tracks in the soft nerve and brain tissue and would become so thoroughly intrenched in the constitution of the brain and mind, as to require long-continued and painful effort to break them up and substitute their opposites. *Character-building is right habit-making;* and to neglect an oft-repeated and long-continued habit, or substitute the opposite, would become much more painful and difficult than to repeat the habitual act.

The habit of happy thought would transform

the commonest life into harmony and beauty. The will is almost omnipotent to determine habits which virtually are omnipotent. The habit of directing a firm and steady will upon those things which tend to produce harmony of thought would produce happiness and contentment even in the most lowly occupations. The will, rightly drilled, can drive out all discordant thoughts, and produce a reign of perpetual harmony.

Superintendent Terhune turned to the pupils in his audience recently, saying:

"This is exactly what I wish to impress upon you now, while your bodies are elastic and your minds plastic: if I could lead all pupils in their teens to study the youthful days of our famous men and women of the past and present, and then lay out their own life work carefully with the highest aims, I would cheerfully relinquish my own life.

"Four habits are especially valuable—punctuality, accuracy, steadiness, and despatch. Without the first, time is wasted; without the second, mistakes the most hurtful to our own credit and interest, and those of others, may be made, without the third, nothing can be well done; and without the fourth, opportunities of great advantage are lost, which it is impossible to recall."

Many an extraordinary man has been made out of a boy of qualities very ordinary except when roused to his best action; but, in order to accomplish it, we must begin with him while he is young. Is it not astonishing what training will do for a rough, uncouth, and even dull lad, if he has good material in him? Yet he must come under the tutelage of a skilled educator before bad habits have become confirmed.

"What we do upon some great occasion," says Lidden, "will depend on what we already are; and what we are will be the result of previous years of self-discipline."

Practically all the achievements of the human race are but the accomplishments of habit. We speak of the power of Gladstone to accomplish so much in a day as something marvellous; but when we analyse that power we find it composed very largely of the results of habit. His mighty momentum was rendered possible only by the law of the power of habit. He was a great bundle of habits, which all his life he was forming. His habit of industry, no doubt, was irksome and tedious at first, but, practised so conscientiously and persistently, it gained such momentum as to astonish the world. His habit of thinking, close, persistent, and strong, made him a power. He formed the habit of accurate, keen observation, allowing nothing to escape his attention, until he could observe more in half a day in London than a score of men who have eyes but see not. Thus he multiplied himself many times. By the habit of accuracy he avoided many a repetition; and so, during his lifetime, he saved years of precious time.

What is put into the first of life is put into the whole of life. If we seldom see much change in people after they get to be twenty-five or thirty years of age, except in going farther in the way they have started, it is a great comfort to think that, when one is young, it is almost as easy to acquire a good habit as a bad one.

If we do not look up, we shall look down. If we do not go forward, we shall go backward. There must be an upward tendency in the life or we shall retrograde towards barbarism.

"I trust everything under God to habit," says Lord Brougham, "upon which, in all ages, the lawgiver as well as the schoolmaster has mainly placed reliance—habit, which makes everything easy, and casts all difficulties upon the deviation from our wonted course."

CHAPTER VI

MONEY, MEANS, AND CONTENT

He that wants money, means, and content, is without three good friends.—SHAKESPEARE.

The great satisfaction coming from wealth is a consciousness of power. Besides this, it opens up the way to a higher delight, meeting one's desires for education and art. The crowning joy of wealth is in the service of society and of mankind.—R. HEBER NEWTON.

WITHOUT independence no one can be a man. Who can do his best work when want is tugging at his heels, or who is hampered, tied down, forever at the mercy of circumstances or of those upon whom he depends for employment? What can be more humiliating for a young man or woman than the sense of being but one day's march ahead of want?

No young man has any right to remain in a position, if it is possible to get out of it, where he will be constantly subjected to the great temptations of poverty. Self-respect demands that he should get out of it. It is his duty to put himself in a position of dignity and independence, where he will not be liable at any moment to be a burden to his friends in case of sickness or of other emergencies.

The pursuit of wealth, say what men may, is not only legitimate, but a duty. If a man is manly and if his fortune be legitimately won, it will increase his influence and multiply his power. The very struggle to attain wealth, if he is careful to guard against its narrowing, dwarfing, demoralising tendencies, will develop his skill, his energy, his thrift, his intelligence and sagacity; will improve his judgment, and train his moral and mental powers. "The soul is trained by the ledger as truly as by the calculus, and can get exercise in an account of sales as in the account of stars." The business man, if he is methodical, is put constantly upon his thoughtfulness; he is in perpetual mental drill from morning till night, if he is a good business man.

A business man must be systematic, orderly, prompt, exact, courteous, considerate, both to those under him and to his patrons; he is constantly in a school of manners; he is constantly put on his good behaviour; and if he is a broad-gauge business man, liberal and magnanimous, and does not allow his business to narrow and contract him, he will constantly improve his manhood, will grow broader, his sympathies deeper, his charities larger.

"If we look among the wrecks of life, in the

poorhouses, among the 'submerged classes,'"
said a wise thinker, " we shall doubtless find, that,
of these unfortunate beings, not one in a thousand was born with riches; on the contrary, many
of them have failed because they were never
properly equipped for the struggle for existence,
by reason of the disadvantages imposed by
poverty."

On every hand we see evidences of pinching,
grinding poverty. We see it in prematurely de-
pressed faces; want stares us in the face every
day in nearly every city; its blighting, blasting
marks are traceable everywhere. We see it in
children who have no childhood; we see it in
suppressed sociability, shadowing bright young
faces; we see its blighting effect upon brilliant
minds. It often means hopelessness to the highest
ambition; it means thwarting of brilliant plans; it
imposes serious obstacles to even the most resolute determination. The poor are ever at the
mercy of circumstances. They cannot be independent, they cannot command their time, nor
can they always afford to live in healthful locali-
ties or in healthful houses. Poverty is a curse;
there is scarcely a redeeming feature about it,
and those who extol its virtues are the last to accept its conditions. Hampered, perhaps, with
debt, in bondage to those on whom one depends
for work, forced to make a dime perform the

proper work of a dollar, it is almost impossible to preserve that dignity and self-respect which enables him to be manly, virtuous, and true. Praise it who will, poverty is narrow, belittling, contracting; there is little hope in it, little prospect in it, little joy in it; it is a terrible strain upon the affections, and often kills love between those who would otherwise live happily. It is the duty of every young man and woman to exert every nerve to get out of its clutches into freedom, where the individuality can find untrammeled expansion.

I believe, with Horace Greeley, that every healthy young man in this country ought to be ashamed of being poor. I would like to fill every young man and woman with an utter dread and horror of poverty. I would like to make them so feel its shame, its constraint, its bitterness, that they would vow to escape its thraldom.

Parents often fail to realise the significance of their children's ambition to earn money. It is a laudable ambition, and should be directed and encouraged, not suppressed. Thousands of boys have been saved from utter worthlessness, for lives of splendid usefulness, by wisely encouraging and fostering this money-making instinct. If a boy be thoroughly honest in his desire for money-making, he is sure to be saved from a thousand temptations and habits of indolence or wildness, and to develop habits of thrift which will influence his entire life.

As Emerson says, "It is mean, low, huckstering trade, that has been the great world developer, the great civilisation lifter." It is very difficult for the rich to be so selfish that the poor cannot enjoy their wealth, for whether they rear it into architecture or put it into elegant carriages and liveries, whether they spend it in costly banquets or dainty fabrics, rare diamonds and precious stones, build costly churches, elegant yachts, summer residences, or city palaces—however they may spend it or use it—thousands of others will see it, enjoy it, and carry away with their eyes a large share of the real value. Each individual is struggling to attain his own ends, but Nature turns all this to the benefit of mankind and the perpetual progress of the race. Each, striving to excel his neighbour, to do the best for himself, contributes to the best result for all. Without this passion for the power, influence, and advantage which money gives, how could nature develop the highest type of man? Without this, whence would come the discipline which industry, perseverance, tact, sagacity, and frugality give?

Money means shoes for bare feet; it means flannels and warm clothing for shivering forms; it means coal for the fire, provisions for the larder,

It means comforts, refinements, education, pictures, books, music, travel; it means a good house and nutritious food; it means independence; it means opportunity to do good; it means the best medical skill; how many poor people lose their lives because they cannot employ a skillful surgeon or physician. Money means rest when we are tired, it means change of climate for the invalid. It means that we are not forced to work through all kinds of weather and exposure, whether we are able or not; it means exemption from the drudgery which dogs the footsteps of the poor.

It is no sin to be rich, nor to wish to be rich; the mistake is in being too eager after riches.

"Get all you can without hurting your soul, your body, or your neighbour," said John Wesley. "Save all you can, cuttting off every needless expense. Give all you can."

"There are some men born with a genius for money-making," says Mathews. "They have the instinct of accumulation. The talent and the inclination to convert dollars into doubloons by bargains or shrewd investments are, in them, just as strongly marked and as uncontrollable as were the ability and the inclination of Shakespeare to produce Hamlet and Othello, of Raphael to paint his cartoons, of Beethoven to compose his symphonies, or Morse to invent an electric telegraph.

As it would have been a gross dereliction of duty, a shameful perversion of gifts, had these latter disregarded the instincts of their genius and engaged in the scramble for wealth, so would Rothschild, Astor, and Peabody have sinned had they done violence to their natures, and thrown their energies into channels where they would have proved dwarfs and not giants."

Money indicates the character of the possessor. It is a great telltale. It betrays tastes, ambitions, and uncovers a hundred secrets. "A right measure in getting," says Arthur Helps, "in saving, spending, giving, taking, lending, borrowing, and bequeathing, would almost argue a perfect man."

I have often thought that, if I were rich, I would like to give a thousand dollars to each of the first hundred people I might meet on the street and see what they would do with it; I would like to trace out the history of each thousand. To the poor boy struggling for an education, it would mean books and a possible college course. To the fast young man it would mean fine clothes, fast horses, pleasure, and a fast life. To a poor girl, it would be support for an invalid mother, clothes, and schooling for sisters. To another it would suggest a wife and home. To the miser it would mean " more hoarding," one thousand more.

"What rubbish do some people talk!" said one who had for years studied economic conditions among all classes. "One would suppose, to hear them, that a bank account, a good home, a tailor-made suit, and well-clad feet, were the insignia of Satan, and that all one needs to designate him as an angel is an empty pocketbook, shabby clothing and little of it, shoeless feet, and ignorance of where the next day's food is coming from. The fact is that too much money, or too much poverty, is apt to be an evil-breeder, but he has not observed wisely, or thought wisely, who has not decided that a man who owns enough of this world's goods to keep him from dirt, debt, and hunger, has a thousand chances of avoiding evil against the one of the man whom the demon of discouragement drags through depths from which it is almost impossible to escape without severe demoralisation of body, mind, and spirit."

"I do not think," said Beecher, "that human nature lays one under a higher stress of temptation through riches than it does through poverty. I know that riches make men proud. Is there no pride among the poor? I know that rich men are self-seeking and vain. Are poor people free from this? I know that rich men may be envious of those in their company, and have ambition to excel each other in mere outward display of riches and amassing the riches themselves. Is there no avaricious desire among the poor? no discontent? no coarse, envious squabbling? I tell you it is not riches, and it is not poverty—it is human nature that lies back of both of them that is dangerous, and that is the trouble."

One of the wisest prayers ever uttered was this: "Give me neither poverty nor riches." Here, as elsewhere, "the middle course is best." To be too rich or too poor is to carry a burden beneath which one must almost inevitably sink to a lower level than that which one of a moderate and adequate fortune will be most likely to occupy. When one's riches become colossal, they are very apt to become unwieldy. They are often like unmanageable horses.

"How do you like your new horses?" one man asked of another. "I've sold them," was the reply. "Sold them! Why, you seemed to like them so much when I last saw you!" "Yes, but I'd just got them then. Almost every time I went out with them they took the bits in their teeth, and ran away with me. They threw me out three times, breaking one finger, dislocating one arm, and bruising me all over. It seemed to be a question of my driving the horses or their driving me, and they were certainly driving me. They were worse than no horses."

With many men, riches "take the bits in their teeth" and run away with their supposed masters, breaking their peace of mind, dislocating their principles, and morally bruising them all over.

Such riches are worse than no riches. But there are curb-bits for unmanageable horses, which make the owner of the steeds master of the situation. So, from firm determination, clear common sense, and deep thought, one should construct a bit which will hold riches in subjection, and make them the managed rather than the manager. The selfish, the miserly, the greedy, the dishonest rich man is controlled by his riches. No man need be taken in hand by his money, yet the man whose wealth keeps him from his family, his required sleep, healthful recreation, and the time to enjoy the legitimate pleasures of life, is thus managed.

A good many people are robbed of all that man should enjoy, by the possession of that which should add so much to their happiness. There is no sadder or more contemptible sight than a greedy, or miserly rich man, who piles up possessions that he may gloat over them, and to whom it is misery to expend a dollar even for his own bodily comfort or soul-evolution.

" About three years ago," said a miser, " by a very odd accident, I fell into a well, and was absolutely within a very few minutes of perishing, before I could prevail upon an unconscionable dog of a labourer, who happened to hear my cries, to help me out for a shilling. The fellow was so rapacious as to insist, for above a quarter of an hour, upon having twenty-five cents; and I verily believe he would not have abated me a single farthing, if he had not seen me at the last gasp, and I determined to die rather than submit to his extortion."

No man can be truly rich who is selfish. Money is like a spring of water in the mountains. It holds the wealth of the valley in its bosom, if it will only expend itself. When it dashes down the mountain, it makes the meadows green and glad with its wealth. Beautiful flowers spring up along its banks and bathe their faces in its sparkling surface. But when we obstruct this beautiful stream, the valleys dry up, the flowers and grass wither and die. So it is with money: while it flows out freely and circulates, it blesses humanity; but when the circulation is interrupted by hoarding it, or squandering and abusing it, it becomes a curse. The heart hardens, the sympathies dry up, the soul becomes a desert.

It is a sad thing to see an old man begging bread, but it is sadder still to see an aged millionaire tottering on the edge of the grave, who has starved his soul to fatten his purse, whose greed for gold has dried up all the noblest springs of his life and stifled his aspirations for the good, the beautiful, and the true. What can be more pitiful than a shrivelled soul with a distended purse? These are not men, but " hungers, thirsts, fevers, and appetites, walking."

"Be charitable before wealth makes thee covetous," says Sir Thomas Browne, "and lose not the glory of the mite. If riches increase, let the mind hold pace with them; and think it not enough to be liberal, but munificent. Diffuse thy beneficence early and while thy treasures call thee master; there may be an atrophy of thy fortunes before that of thy life, and thy wealth be cut off before that hour when all men shall be poor."

"How I would like to exchange places with John Jacob Astor," exclaimed a New York man to a friend with whom he was discussing the subject of wealth. "Would you be willing to take care of all his property—ten or fifteen million dollars—merely for your board and clothing?" "No," was the indignant reply; "do you take me for a fool?" "Well," rejoined the other, "that is all Mr. Astor himself gets out of it; he's 'found,' and that's all. The houses, the warehouses, the ships, the farms, which he counts by the hundred, and is often obliged to take care of, are for the accommodation of others." "But then," said the first speaker, "he has the income or rents of this large property, five or six hundred thousand dollars a year." "Yes, but he can do nothing with his income but build more houses and warehouses and ships, or loan money on mortgages for the convenience of others. He's

' found,' and you can make nothing else out of it."

" The pursuit of wealth for the wealth alone," says a wise writer, " is unworthy the life devotion of man. The man who saves much money at the cost of his honour, his manhood, and life's richest experiences of heart and mind is most improvident. Money is good only for what it will provide. Let no young man set his heart upon money alone and despise those greater things which make life worth living."

He is the richest man who absorbs into himself the most of the best in the world in which he lives, and gives the most of himself to others. He is the richest man in whose possessions others feel richest. To be rich is to have a strong, robust constitution; to have a hearty appreciation of the beautiful in nature; to have access to the masterpieces of art, science, and literature; to have companionship with great men and women; to have a past which haunts not with remorse; to have a mind both liberally stored and contented.

CHAPTER VII

OCCASION'S FORELOCK

But on occasion's forelock watchful wait.
MILTON.

THE whole period of youth," said Ruskin, " is one essentially of formation, edification, instruction. There is not an hour of it but is trembling with destinies—not a moment of it when, once passed, the appointed work can ever happen again, or the neglected blow be struck on the cold iron."

In an important sense, men are to make their own opportunities. Lincoln did. Henry Wilson did. George Stephenson did. Napoleon did. There never was a man who achieved peculiar eminence who did not do it by advancing upon a path that he made as he went along. What is an opportunity for another is not perhaps my personal opportunity, for it does not appeal to me. I must primarily bear about within myself the ideas, purposes and energies by which I am to achieve the mastery. Individual capacity must be behind everything.

Until he finds what is likely to be his life calling, one is to make the most of his present chance, and keep his eyes open and his hands free. To illustrate: Take the case of George Pullman. He began his life work upon a salary of forty dollars a year as store clerk. This and his board was all that he received for three years. Then this was given up, and he did joiner work. Then he sought employment as a mover of buildings. Working at this carefully and energetically, he was finally employed by the State of New York to remove several large warehouses along the line of the Erie Canal; and, when this work was completed, he went to Chicago, and there engaged in the same business. The entire city was to be raised eight feet in order to introduce a sewerage system. Pullman did his work so well that he had no end of orders. It was while working upon the Chicago buildings that he made plans for improving the rude sleeping cars that had recently been introduced on the Chicago and Alton Railway. He could foresee the future of " parlours " and " bedrooms " upon wheels. He began by building a most luxurious car, costing more than four times as much as any previously made. Thenceforth he gave the main energies of his life to making the " Pullman cars." Yet in his late, as well as his early career, whenever he saw a new opportunity by which he could forward his main end of acquiring capital and establishing himself in still more productive business, he at once adapted himself to the circumstances of the hour, so far as it could be done without impairing the substantial unity of his principal business.

Storekeeping did not appeal to Pullman as his opportunity, nor did ordinary carpentry. To Marshall Field, however, storekeeping did appeal. It proved to be his opportunity. He was equal to it, and succeeded where others failed. It is often difficult to see any difference between the men who succeed and those who fail. They often start out with the same amount of capital, and, apparently, with equal advantages; but, although, perhaps, not noticeable by the average observer, one has a little more energy, a little more politeness, is a little more accommodating, attends a little more closely to details, is more prompt, gets to the store or the office a little earlier and stays a little later, takes a paper or two and a magazine, and reads books and papers along the line of his business or profession, and above all has a clearer business perception; these are not seeming trifles, they make all the difference between success and failure.

Here was Chauncey Jerome. His education was limited to three months in the district school each year until he was ten, when his father took him into his blacksmith shop at Plymouth, Connecticut, to make nails. Money was a scarce article with young Jerome. He once chopped a load of wood for one cent, and often chopped by moonlight for neighbours at less than a dime a load. His father died when the boy was eleven years old, and his mother was forced to send Chauncey out, with tears in his eyes and a little bundle of clothes in his hand, to earn a living on a farm. His new employer kept him at work early and late chopping down trees, his shoes sometimes full of snow, for he had no boots until he was nearly twenty-one. At fourteen he was apprenticed for seven years to a carpenter, who gave him only board and clothes for his wages. Several times, during his apprenticeship, he carried his tools thirty miles on his shoulder to his work at different places. After he had learned his trade, he frequently walked thirty miles to a job with his kit upon his back. One day he heard people talking of Eli Terry, of Plymouth, who had undertaken to make two hundred clocks in one lot. " He'll never live long enough to finish them," said one. " If he should," said another, " he could not possibly sell so many. The very idea is ridiculous." Chauncey pondered long over this rumour, for it had been his dream to become a great clock-maker. He tried his hand, at the first opportunity, and soon learned to make a wooden clock. When he got an order to make twelve, at twelve dollars apiece, he thought his fortune was made.

One night he happened to think that a cheap clock could be made of brass as well as of wood, and would not shrink, swell, or warp appreciably in any climate. He acted on the idea, and became the first great manufacturer of brass clocks. He made millions at the rate of six hundred a day, exporting them to all parts of the globe.

One must first of all get a footing in that which he is fit for. He must early discover what that is. Professor Sargent of Harvard could see that it was to him a vantage ground when, as a student, he got a footing in the Bowdoin college gymnasium. He followed up his advantage, and he is, at this moment, the most eminent physical instructor in America. " To seize upon an opportunity is of the utmost importance," the Professor remarked in a recent interview; " even though the remuneration may seem small and inadequate. It is not to the value of his service to which a young man should look, but to the opportunity offered." He began work upon a salary of eighty-three cents a day.

Collis P. Huntington, the great railway man, was the son of a Connecticut farmer. He abandoned the opportunities of the farm, and peddled clocks along the Erie Canal. In California he opened a hardware store. He united with Leland Stanford in the construction of a railroad. With him one thing always led to another. He made the most of the opportunity he had; and, when he could clearly see another that was manifestly better, he took it upon the instant. So did John Jacob Astor and Peter Cooper, Cornelius Vanderbilt and Philip D. Armour, Andrew Carnegie and John D. Rockefeller.

The difference between men, in a business point of view, is largely a difference in their perceptive and executive powers—the ability to see and to act. There is seldom want of opportunity, but there frequently is a want of capacity to discern it and to achieve success in it. There is, for example, a difference in blacksmiths. When Ichabod Washburn was apprentice to a blacksmith in Worcester, Massachusetts, he was a singularly bashful boy; yet when he found that no good wire was made in the United States, and that one house in England had the monopoly of making steel wire for pianos, he quietly determined that he would himself make the best wire in the world, and that he would then contrive ways and means to manufacture it in enormous quantities. The bashful boy had his eyes wide open. He saw a great opportunity, and such was his executive ability that what he thought, he actually did. His wire became the standard everywhere. His business finally increased to such an extent that he made twelve tons of iron wire every day, employing the services of seven hundred men. And the great fortune he acquired he largely gave away in charities to make the world better.

Colonel William L. Strong, of Ohio, was far-sighted. When he was earning a salary of three thousand dollars a year, a great woolen merchant invited him to take a position in his store at twelve hundred a year; yet Strong was far-sighted enough, or long-headed enough, as we say, to see that in this business was an opportunity worth far more than the three thousand a year, and he promptly accepted the diminution of eighteen hundred a year in his salary. Later he became the head of that woolen house.

It is not uncommon for a youth to wander about here and there without at first discerning what is life's great opportunity for him. Erskine, the great English advocate, spent four years in the navy, in early life; and then, in the hope of more rapid promotion, he joined the army. Here he served more than two years, without once suspecting that some other destiny was in store for him. Yet one fortunate day he attended a court, out of curiosity, in the town where his regiment was quartered. The presiding judge, an acquaintance, invited Erskine to sit near him, and he said to the youth that the pleaders at the bar that morning were among the most eminent lawyers of Great Britain. No sooner did Erskine hear what they said than he mentally took their measure, and he believed that he himself could excel them one and all. In an instant he decided to study law; it was in him, indeed, to excel them all; and he became one of the greatest forensic orators of the nation.

There are more persons who see opportunities than there are who both see and seize them. The forth-putting of power is not common. Young people lack ambition. They fall readily into beaten paths. Not infrequently they say: " This would be a good chance, or that." Yet they have not the courage, or confidence in their own powers to take advantage of either chance. They do not form a purpose till it is too late. The opportunity goes by without their utilising it.

" Thirty years ago, Mr. H., a nurseryman in New York State, left home for a day or two. It was rainy weather, and not a season for sales; but a customer arrived from a distance, hitched his horse, and went into the kitchen of a farm-house, where two lads were cracking nuts.

" ' Is Mr. H. at home?'

" ' No, sir,' said the eldest, Joe, hammering at a nut.

" ' When will he be back?'

" ' Dunno, sir; mebbe not for a week.'

" The other boy, Jim, jumped up and followed the man out. ' The men are not here, but I can show you the stock,' said he, with such a bright, courteous manner that the stranger, who was a little irritated, stopped and followed him through the nursery, examining the trees, and left his order.

"'You have sold the largest bill that I have had this season, Jim,' his father said to him, greatly pleased, on his return home.

"'I'm sure,' said Joe, 'I'm as willing to help as Jim, if I'd thought in time.'

"A few years afterwards, these two boys were left, by the father's failure and death, with two or three hundred dollars each. Joe bought an acre or two near home. He has worked hard but is still a poor, discontented man.

"Jim bought an emigrant's ticket to Colorado, hired as a cattle driver for a couple of years, and with his wages he bought land at forty cents an acre, built himself a house and married. His herds of cattle were numbered by the thousand. The land he bought he cut up for town lots, and he is ranked as one of the wealthiest men of the State.

"'I might have done like Jim,' said his brother, lately, 'if I'd thought in time. There's as good stuff in me as in him.'

"'There's as good stuff in this loaf of bread as in any I ever made,' said his wife, 'but nobody can eat it; there's not enough yeast in it.'

"The retort, though disagreeable, was applicable. The quick, wide-awake energy which acts as leaven in a character is partially natural. But it can be inculcated by parents, and acquired by a boy if he chooses to keep his eyes open and act promptly and boldly in every emergency."

History furnishes thousands of examples of men who have seized occasions to accomplish results deemed impossible by those less resolute. Prompt decision and whole-souled action sweep the world before them.

When William Phipps, a young shepherd boy from Maine, who had learned the ship carpenter's trade, was one day walking the streets in Boston, he overheard some sailors talking about a Spanish ship that had been wrecked off the Bahama Islands, which was supposed to have a great amount of money on board. He determined to find it. He set out at once, and after many hardships discovered the lost treasure.

What the sailors talked about, he did. He had the executive quality. His ability to act promptly made him a colonial governor of Massachusetts.

It is always so. John Knight, of Guatemala City, was a slave in Alabama in 1860. Gaining his freedom, he became a wharf labourer for a firm that handled Central American fruits, and this led him to think of the possibility of becoming himself a fruit grower. This idea he carried out, while others who worked with him perhaps never thought it open to a wharf labourer to do it. He secured from the government of Guatemala 50,000 acres of land, and then arranged with the New Orleans fruit dealers to buy $2,000,000 worth a year of Guatemala fruits. Since then he has become a coffee grower and a dealer in mahogany logs, and he is to-day one of the richest and most powerful men in Central America. His executive quality matched his perceptive faculty.

The pre-eminently successful men have been those who actually improved what opportunities they saw.

James F. Ryder, a photographer in Cleveland, Ohio, happened one day to read in a German paper of a new process practised by the artists of Bohemia—by which they touched up a negative with fine instruments, thus removing any imperfections. Reading this, he immediately sent to Bohemia for an artist, and at length succeeded in bringing the art of Bohemia into his own service. He seized his opportunity by the forelock, and secured the best aid possible in his business, and then he brought to bear the forces of an energetic mind to advertise and extend his business. In a photographic exhibition in Boston, Mr. Ryder took the prize for the best work in America.

Professor Benedict was a teacher of Latin. Upon first hearing the click of a typewriter he cried to himself, "Eureka." He at once understood the possibilities of the invention. Throwing his Latin away, he began to manufacture the Remington typewriter, so useful, and to him so remunerative.

A recent authority upon manufactures has told us that the great plants of Europe are, many of them, hampered by an unreadiness to make the most of their opportunities; while in America, if a man has a good thing, he fills the world with his goods.

"Vigilance in watching opportunity," said Phelps; "tact and daring in seizing upon opportunity; force and persistence in crowding opportunity to its utmost of possible achievement—these are the martial virtues which must command success."

When you once see your opportunity, you are to think for it, plan for it, work for it, live for it—throw your mind, might, strength, heart, and soul into it, and success will crown you. The successful men of to-day are men of one overmastering idea, men of single and intense purpose.

"The best men," says E. H. Chapin, "are not those who have waited for chances, but who have taken them; besieged the chance; conquered the chance; and made chance the servitor."

How it shortens the road to success to make
early a wise choice of one's occupation, to be
started on the road of a proper career while
young and full of hope, while the animal spirits
are high and one's enthusiasm is wide awake.

> "I hear a voice you cannot hear,
>   Which says I must not stay;
> I see a hand you cannot see,
>   Which beckons me away."

As a rule, in the early part of life, when the
perceptive powers are perhaps little developed,
and when one's energies are spent in play or need-
ful work, the notion is entertained by many people that success is something far away, to be
found, perhaps, in some other community, or
when one is connected with different associates.
It is not in their thoughts that they can succeed
where they are.

Distance seems to have a great charm for
youth, especially for boys. They are all looking
for great chances, for unusual openings. It is
difficult to convince them that almost all of the
successful men of the country found their opportunities right where their duties placed them, and
did not succeed by running away to some other
city or country.

Very few boys, to-day, though they live in a
paradise of good opportunities, think they have

any chance. If they could only get to Chicago, San Francisco, New York, or some other large city, they feel sure they could succeed, but they cannot see any opportunity on the farm or in a little country town.

If youths would only realise that every little task in the store or on the farm is an opportunity to cultivate the very principles upon which every success must stand, to cultivate despatch and system, to enlarge the observation, to practise good manners, to learn the value of politeness and courtesy; if they could only realise that these are all stepping-stones to something higher; that the ladder upon which they must climb to success, if at all, is close to them; that every task rightly done will advance them a step on their way, they would already be far on the road to success.

Boys are always dreaming about genius, of what it can accomplish, and wondering why they do not have it. They do not realise that the great majority of men who have risen to be superintendents, managers, and proprietors of great stores, found their first opportunity in sweeping the floors of those very stores.

Remember, young men, that the chances are that the steps to your promotion are right where you are, not somewhere else. If you fill your present position, whatever it may be, full to overflowing; if you are faithful, careful, and prudent;

if you study the needs of the next higher step above you, you may soon take that step.

Most young men exaggerate the advantages of large centers. They think, because they are on a farm or in a country town, they have no opportunities. But the fact is, many of the most successful men in our history have found their opportunities in just such places. It is true that later in life, many of them moved to large cities for wider fields, but they got their start in the country. Energy, push, and determination will bring openings even to very small places. If one is hungry for an education, if he longs for self-improvement, he will find ways of getting either in a country town.

The small towns are healthier, quieter, and afford a better chance to learn to think. There are fewer distractions and exactions on one's time, while the nervous strain is infinitely less. The excitement, the competition, the hurry and strife of the larger cities ruin many a fine constitution and bring failure to many who would have succeeded in smaller places. I am not saying anything against the large centres, as they afford many opportunities of culture which cannot be found elsewhere, but I do say there are many advantages in the smaller places which compensate for their deficiencies in other directions. A robust physique is the foundation of all success, and a city is a poor place to build up a good physical foundation.

Young men are to remember that their truest wealth is at their very feet, awaiting only the stalwart arm and dauntless will to seek and find. In themselves, and in the homely surroundings of to-day, lie hid the treasures for which, elsewhere, they would seek in vain.

Is it not possible that you have an opportunity at your own door? Upon learning that trout commanded a dollar a pound at the summer hotels, a New Hampshire man, living near by, purchased a few books upon fish culture, and then stocked the waters that ran through his mountain farm; and he earned within a few years much more from his living waters than he had ever been able to secure from his rocky lands.

"Brother Steve and I have decided to go West," said a young farmer, " We shall take up a big farm and raise something worth while."

" Why not raise something worth while on the land you have? " asked his wife. " I shall not go West with you, till we have honestly tried to make our Eastern land yield us a good living."

The young man, thus set to thinking, decided to plant a large patch of unused ground with strawberries and supply the neighbours with the fruit. The berries proved so remunerative that he began to improve and put to use other patches of land. He has now one of the best-paying fruit farms in his State.

A Yankee who was slowly recovering from a long illness, was engaged in whittling a piece of soft pine one day, and he made from it a toy for his little baby boy at play in the yard. He did his work so well that all the boys in the neighbourhood beset him to make toys for them, and he soon found himself in the business of retailing home-made toys throughout the school district where he lived. Consequently, as his health improved, he carried on a very extensive toy business, his goods going far and wide.

It was a Massachusetts soldier in the Civil War who observed a bird hulling rice. He took the bill of that bird for his model, and invented a hulling machine which revolutionised the rice business.

Are not the opportunities of life at your own door? A Maine man was called in from his hay field to wash clothes for his invalid wife. He had never realised what it was to wash before. Finding the method slow and laborious, he invented a washing machine and made a fortune. An observing barber in New Jersey invented clippers, and became rich. It is the small, inexpensive invention, for which there is a great demand, that is most profitable. The inventor of a patent for fastening kid gloves made several hundred thousand dollars out of it. The inventor of the collar clasp has an income of $20,000 a year in royalties. A sleeve button appliance has made $50,000 in five years for its patentee. A woman twisted a hairpin to make it stay in more securely, and her husband observed it, and went into the manufacture of crinkled hair-pins, and made his fortune out of it.

It is useless for you to say, " I cannot do this." You can at least keep your eyes open and cultivate your powers of perception, and see what you can do. A woman at Penobscot, Maine, now manufactures more than twelve thousand dozen mittens. " I began business," she said, " in 1864, in a little room about fifteen by twenty, upon a capital of forty dollars. I lived in the country where there was little work, and many women's hands were ready to knit. During the first year I did not use twenty-five pounds of yarn. Yet I ultimately secured 1,500 people in the farm towns to do my knitting. In 1882 I began to buy machines, and the work I used to do at a cost of twenty-five cents a pair is now done at six." The difference between Mrs. A. C. Condon, who did this work, and her neighbours was this: She had it in her to do actually what others merely thought of.

A bright American woman who had a piece of swamp land was asked what she could do with it.

"That land is only fit for frogs to live on."
"Why, frogs shall live upon it; I will raise frogs,
and send them to the markets." And this she has
done so successfully that she has bought all the
adjoining swamps and enlarged her frog farm;
and she now sends a large supply of this peculiar
produce to the markets that have a demand for it.

A young woman named Maxwell, of Kansas
City, started a boot-blacking enterprise, that she
might obtain a living by it. She employed the
boot-blacks, and established them at suitable points
throughout the city. Very soon she found herself earning five or six times as much net as she
could have done by teaching school. When she
secured a surplus above what she needed for her
ordinary expenses, the extra money she received
was devoted to the relief of the unfortunate; and
she systematically assisted the boot-blacks and
street arabs, who became her fast friends. Several hours a day she devotes to the supervision of
her business, and her popular manners and winning ways have secured for her an ample patron-
age. The charitable work she has conducted has
been of great service to the poorest of the poor in
her own city, and her example has proved widely
useful.

In all these cases, there was at the outset no
call for capital, or distant travel, or perhaps of
preparation unduly long. In the highest achieve-

ments of life, one's success usually bears an exact proportion to the preparation that has been made for it.

When George W. Childs was twelve years old, he went to work in Philadelphia, where he received money enough to pay his board and lodging, and have fifty cents left, being twenty-five dollars a year for all his expenses outside bed and board. Yet it was an opportunity, and he fitted himself for it, and made the most of it.

"I did not do merely the work I was required to do," he said, "but I did all that I could, and put my whole heart into it. I wanted my employer to feel that I was more useful to him than he expected me to be. I was not afraid to make fires, clean and sweep, and to perform what some gentlemen nowadays consider as menial work and therefore beneath them. It was while I was working here as an errand boy that I employed such opportunity as I had to read books; and I attended book sales at night, so as to learn the market value of books and anything else that might be useful thereafter in my business in a bookseller's shop. I fixed my ambition high, so that I might at least be always tending upward.

"I lived near a theatre, and many of the actors knew me, so that I might have gone in and witnessed the performances. Other boys did it, and I would have liked to do it; but I thought it over, and concluded that I would not, and I never did. A young man should not yield to any temptation to relax his efforts in attending to his business, in order to amuse himself. At least that was the way I looked at it. I was always cheerful, and took an interest in my work, and took pleasure in doing it well.

" When after some time I had an office in the Public Ledger Building, I said to myself, ' Some time I will own that paper'; and I directed my work in such a way that when the time came I was able to buy it, and I was also able to manage it properly."

The point that I would make in regard to the preparation of the youth for the opportunities of life is further illustrated by a story in the " Youth's Companion," of John Grant, who worked in a hardware store at two dollars a week. His employers said to him, upon entering the store: " Make yourself useful by becoming acquainted with all the details of this business; and, as fast as you prove yourself capable, we will recognise your services in some way."

Several weeks later, young Grant, who had been closely watching, observed that his employer always attended to the checking of the bills of imported foreign goods. These were in French and German. He set to work to study the bills, and to learn commercial French and German, in which they were written. One day when his employer was much pressed for time, Grant offered to do the checking for him; and he did it so well that the next bills which came in were handed to him as a matter of course.

A month later, he was called into the office and interviewed by both the active members of the firm. The senior member said: "In my forty years of experience in this business you are the first boy who has seen this opportunity and improved it. I always had to do the work until Mr. Williams came, and one reason why he became a member of the firm was because he could attend to this part of the business. We want you to take charge of the foreign goods. It is an important position; in fact, it is a matter of necessity that we have someone who can do this work. You, only, of the twenty young men we have here, saw the place and fitted yourself for it."

Grant's pay was advanced to ten dollars per week; in five years he received eighteen hundred dollars salary, and had been sent to France and Germany. "John Grant," said his employer, "will probably become a member of the firm at thirty. He saw the opportunity, and fitted himself for it at some sacrifice; but it paid. It always pays."

It was a saying of Disraeli that the secret of success in life is for a man to be ready for his opportunity when it comes.

" What we call a turning point," says Arnold, " is simply an occasion which sums up and brings to a result previous training. Accidental circumstances are nothing except to men who have been trained to take advantage of them."

It is a common saying to-day among employers that the young men who come to them for work are not prepared for the opportunities which arise in connection with the business in which they wish to be engaged; and, if they are not prepared, when the opportunity arises they fail to secure what might easily fall to them.

A paper of recent date says of a navy yard: "Some forty labourers will be discharged from the department of construction and repair, by reason of lack of work at present." But in the very next column, in strong lines, this appeared: " Good jobs for the right men," with the subhead, " Government examiners failed to find master workmen for directing three kinds of navy-yard work." Not a single one of the many applicants who took the examinations for the positions of master machinist for shop work, master machinist for float work, and master coppersmith, came up to the government qualifications for the positions, and none was recommended for the vacant places by the examining board.

Opportunity is latent in the very foundation of human society. Opportunity is everywhere about

us. But the preparation to seize upon the opportunity, and to make the most of it, is to be made
by everyone for himself; and for himself he will
be self-made or never made. "Occasion," says
President Garfield, "may be the bugle call that
summons an army to battle, but the blast of the
bugle call can never make soldiers nor win battles." What is life but a training school? And
what is the training but self-training.

This is an age of marvellous material development and astounding enterprise. A new civilisation
is holding up glittering prizes to the twentieth century youth with pluck and determination. The
next century will call loudly for trained men and
women who can do one thing as well as it can be
done. It will offer no prizes to the smatterer or
the man or woman who can do a little of everything. Finely trained and well-disciplined aspi-
rants only will win twentieth century laurels. (The
prizes will be greater than in any previous century, but the youth who would win must have a
better general education; he must have a special
knowledge in his particular line.) *This is an age of specialists*

Avenues greater in number, wider in extent,
easier of access than ever before existed, stand
open to the sober, frugal, energetic and able
mechanic, to the educated youth, to the office boy
and to the clerk—avenues through which they can
reap greater successes than were ever before

within the reach of these classes within the history of the world. A little while ago there were only three or four professions—now there are fifty. And of trades, where there was one there are a hundred now.

The opportunities of the race have increased more in the last century, perhaps, than in all previous time. This tremendous revolution in the world of invention, of discovery, of improvement, and such rapid strides in the arts and sciences, have opened a thousand new fields for endeavour, a thousand new wants to be supplied, so that it is simply a question of climbing a little higher in order to find room enough for the most ambitious and progressive. " Go up higher " is the voice which calls from the future.

The world is all gates, all opportunities to him who will use them. What is life itself but opportunity to broaden, deepen, heighten the God-given faculties within, to round out one's whole being into symmetry, harmony, and beauty? Is not the highest opportunity of life the opportunity of service? " How magnificent the opportunity which awaits the world's youth to-day, for self-invest-ment in enterprises with an intellectual and moral outlook—to make money for this, to live for this! "

CHAPTER VIII

SUBJUNCTIVE HEROES

THE world is full of just-a-going-to-be heroes—subjunctive heroes who might, could, would, or should be this or that, but for certain obstacles or discouragements. They long for success, one and all, but they want it at a discount. The " one price " for all is too high. They covet the golden round in the ladder, but do not like to climb the difficult steps by which alone it can be reached. They long for victory, but shrink from the fight. They are forever looking for soft places and smooth surfaces where there will be the least resistance, forgetting that the very friction which retards a train upon the track, and counteracts a fourth of all the engine's power, is essential to its locomotion. Grease the track, and, though the engine puffs and the wheels revolve, the train will not move an inch.

That was a lazy fellow who complained that he could not find bread for his family. " Neither can I," said an honest labourer; " I have to work for all the bread I get."

The Romans arranged the seats, in their two

temples to Virtue and Honour, so that one could not enter the second without passing through the first. Such is always the order of advance— virtue, toil, honour. *Laboremus* (let us work) was the last word of the dying Roman Emperor Severus, as his soldiers gathered around him. Labor, achievement, was the great Roman motto, and the secret of her conquest of the world. The greatest generals returned from their triumphs to the plough. Agriculture was held in great esteem, and it was considered the highest compliment to call a Roman a great agriculturist. Many of their family names were derived from agricultural terms, as Cicero from *cicero,* a chick-pea, and Fabius from *faba,* a bean. The rural tribes held the foremost rank in the early days of the empire. City people were regarded as an indolent, nerveless race. A mighty nation was Rome while industry led her people. When her great conquest of wealth and multitude of slaves placed her citizens above the necessity of labour, that moment her glory began to fade; vice and corruption, induced by idleness, doomed the proud city to an ignominious history.

Queen Victoria did not spend her time in luxurious ease. She was an indefatigable worker in the great affairs of state which were under her control. She acquired several European languages, and in her later years learned Hindustani, because it is the vernacular of millions of her subjects.

Whether you are a monarch or a peasant, an average man or woman, there is always something wrong about you if you look upon manual labour as degrading. A Baltimore Bonaparte surprised a friend by carrying home a broom. " Why, it belongs to me," was his reply to the look of incredulity. A Washington correspondent wrote home: " Yesterday I saw General Sam Houston, once governor of Texas, now a senator, carrying, like Lord Napier, his own small bundle of a clean shirt and towel, a piece of soap, and a hair-brush." Lord Tenterden was proud to point out to his son the shop where his father had shaved for a penny. Louis Philippe once said he was the only sovereign in Europe fit to govern, since he could black his own boots.

Rome's glory had already begun to fade when it was asserted, by her greatest orator, that " All artisans are engaged in a disgraceful occupation." To Greece it was a shame that Aristotle should say: " The best regulated cities will not permit a mechanic to be a citizen, for it is impossible for one who leads the life of a mechanic, or hired servant, to practise a life of virtue. Some were born to be slaves." There came One mightier than Cicero, or Aristotle, whose magnificent life and example forever lifted the ban from labour, and redeemed it from disgrace; he gave to it significance, and dignity to the most menial service.

Young men who have a vulgar horror of commerce, who have perhaps been trained with the idea that it is not genteel to engage in it, shut their eyes to the fact that usefulness is the measure of greatness. A situation in a government office, a bank, or with a great company, according to their conception, is the thing for a gentleman. They will work and wait for custom-house clerkships such a length of time as would suffice to secure them far better positions in counting-houses; and they will settle into service for life, instead of rising to independence. The professions have great charms for some of this class. In their dislike of business or manual labour, they think they can make an easier living, and take a better position, in one of the liberal callings. They imagine that ignorance or incompetence has a better chance in a profession than in commerce; that in the one a decorous sham has nothing to fear, while the other requires work and ability. You will know them by their utter want of enthusiasm. They are idle while they are students, and throw their books one side as soon as they have passed their examinations.

It is men of this class, who have a false ideal of work—if they can be said to have any ideal at all—against whom Montalembert has so eloquently warned us, pointing out the danger of stimulating and propagating the passion for salaries and government employment, which saps all national spirit of independence, and in some countries makes a whole people a mere crowd of servile solicitors for place.

Never feel above your business. All legitimate occupations are respectable. It is not your honest work that has power to degrade you, but the spirit in which you approach it. If you are one of those of whom Gibbon says, "He well remembers he has a salary to receive, and only forgets he has a duty to perform," you are likely to be of small use to your employers or to yourself. Do not choose your life work solely for the money that you can make by it. "Light work, but the heart must be in it!" So read an advertisement in an English paper when a curate was wanted. Heavy work, but the heart in it—that is the story of many a life considered successful. The "light work" men, as a rule, are not the men who subdue kingdoms, little or large. It is a contemptible estimate of an occupation to regard it as a mere means of making a living. The Creator might have given us our bread ready-made. He might have kept us in luxurious Eden forever; but He had a grander and nobler end in view, when He created man, than the mere satisfaction of his animal appetites and passions. There was a divinity within man, which the luxuries of Eden could never develop. There was an inestimable blessing in that curse which drove him from the garden, and compelled him forever to earn his bread by the sweat of his brow. It was not without significance that the Creator concealed our highest happiness and greatest good beneath the sternest difficulties, and made their attainment conditional upon a struggle for existence. "Our motive power is always found in what we lack."

"There is no road to success," says Munger, "but through a clear, strong purpose; which underlies character, culture, position, attainment of whatever sort."

"It is only by labour," wrote Ruskin, "that thought can be made healthy, and only by thought that labour can be made happy; and the two cannot be separated with impunity."

Why does a bit of canvas with the "Angelus" on it bring one hundred and twenty-five thousand dollars, while that of another artist brings but a dollar? It is because Millet put one hundred and twenty-five thousand dollars' worth of brains and labour into his canvas, while the other man put only a dollar's worth into his.

A blacksmith makes five dollars' worth of iron into horseshoes, and gets ten dollars for them. A cutler makes the same iron into knives, and gets two hundred dollars. A machinist makes the same iron into needles, and gets sixty-eight hundred dollars. A watchmaker takes it and makes it into mainsprings, and gets two hundred thousand dollars; or into hair-springs, and gets two million dollars, sixty times the value of the same weight of gold.

So it is with our life material, which is given us at birth. Do something with it we must. We cannot throw it away, for even idleness leaves its curse upon it. One young man works up his into objects of beauty and utility. Another botches and spoils his without purpose or aim until, perhaps, late in life, he comes to his senses and tries to patch up the broken and wasted pieces; but it is a sorry apology to leave, in payment for a life of magnificent possibilities. "The ploughman may be a Cincinnatus, or a Washington, or he may be brother to the clod he turns."

In the Louvre is a picture, by Murillo, of the interior of a convent kitchen, in which the workers are white-winged angels instead of ordinary mortals. "One is putting the kettle on to boil, and one is lifting up a pail of water with heavenly grace, and one is at the kitchen dresser, reaching up for plates. So the commonest things of everyday life are worthy of the attention even of angels. It is the spirit of the act, and not the act itself, which gives it character. If it be humdrum, it is because we make it so in the doing."

It is the ideal in labour that makes the difference between your work and that of your neighbours. Some increasing purpose runs through your life, year by year, widening or narrowing your thoughts " with the process of the suns." According as you broaden or grow narrower, your work is dignified or lessened in dignity. Are you a working mason? Can you see " poetry in bricks and mortar?" Or only so many mugs of beer and pipes of tobacco? Are you a book-keeper? Can you read between the columns of your laboriously calculated pages—" By my faithfulness and endurance to-day I have made myself by a little a better man?" Are you a school teacher, weary with your daily round? Can you say " I shall be more tactful and patient some other day because I have seen a child so patient to-day?"

" To those who look at their work only from the outside, on the material and often commonplace side, it appears gloomy and colourless. It seems to have no meaning. It has neither charm nor value. It is like looking at the windows of a church from the outside, at the windows of old cathedrals that have grown dark and dusty with time. Everything is lost beneath a monotonous, formless gray. But cross the threshold, and penetrate to the interior. Immediately the colours stand forth, the lines are seen, the tracery becomes evident. There is a marvellous play of the sun through the glass, a feast for the eyes, a triumph of art. This is the case with human activity. We must look at it from the inside. We must try to penetrate sufficiently far into our career, our vocation, to perceive, through the forms—which from without seemed dim—the effects of a light which falls from the eternal heights."

He who can look upon his work from the inside, who regards it not as a curse, but as a privilege, is independent, whether he be in the lap of fortune or out of fortune's graces. He has something to live for, whatever the means he has to live by; and by so much the more does he approach the stature of a perfect man.

CHAPTER IX

THE PRICE OF SUCCESS

No mortal thing can bear so high a price
But that with mortal thing it may be bought.
                                    SIR WALTER RALEIGH.

THE gods sell anything and to everybody at a fair price," said Emerson. Examine the biographies of a thousand men who have achieved the work they wished to accomplish, and you will find fresh evidence that the gods sell everything at that fair price, nothing without it. You will never find success "marked down."

Having decided what is to be your life work, and that if you prepare for it your work will be worth more, you find yourself confronted by the question, "How much are you willing to pay for success in your undertaking?" You can have what you desire, if you will pay the price.

Were you cast into prison like Galileo for presuming to find out a few scientific facts, could you experiment with a straw in your cell? Had you invented a machine, and made it perfect beyond almost any other at its first introduction, only to find, with Eli Whitney or Elias Howe, that those

whom it was intended to bless refused to use it at
first, and later tried to steal it, would it dampen
your inventive ardour? Could you plod on with
enthusiasm after seeing a mob tear down the mill
you had erected for the use of your machinery?
Could you wait eight years for a patent on teleg-
raphy, like Samuel F. B. Morse, and then almost
fight for a chance to introduce it? Could you
invent a hay-tedder, and then pay a farmer for
trying it on his hay, because he said it would
" knock the seeds off? " Would you, if you had
invented McCormick's reaper, have the persistence to introduce it into England against the
opposition of the press, which ridiculed it as " a
cross between an Astley chariot, a wheelbarrow,
and a flying machine "? Would you live in the
woods, as Audubon did for years to reproduce his
drawings of North American birds, after they
had been destroyed by Norway rats? After
acquiring a fortune, could you give up your well-
earned leisure, devote years of almost hopeless
drudgery, and risk all your wealth, amid the
scoffs of men, in a seemingly futile attempt to bind
two continents together by an electric cord, like
Cyrus W. Field?

What was the price Napoleon paid before he
secured recognition? He waited seven weary
years for an appointment, and during his enforced
leisure he supplemented what was considered a

thorough military education by further intense study—by researches and reflections which enabled him to teach the art of war to veterans who had never dreamed of his novel combinations.

Was it worth while for Michael Angelo, when painting the Sistine Chapel, to carry mortar for the frescoers up long ladders in order to catch suggestions from the words of the workmen, to sleep in his clothes, and to eat of bread kept within reach that he might lose no time for meals or dress? Angelo kept a block of marble in his bedroom, that he might get up in the night and work when he could not sleep. His favourite device was an old man in a go-cart, with an hour-glass upon it, bearing this inscription: "Still I am learning." Even after he was blind, he would ask to be wheeled into the Belvedere, to examine the statues with his hands. Keeping eternally at it was the price he was willing to pay for his art.

Would your passion for art give you nerve like that of Vernet to sketch the towering wave on the Mediterranean that threatened to engulf your vessel?

Would your patience suffice to practise, as Handel did upon his harpsichord, until every key was hollowed by your fingers to resemble the bowl of a spoon?

" There is but one price for honourable distinction," says Thayer; "we can take it or leave it. The irresolute, limp young man who expects to find success 'at a bargain' some day, as merchants bandy their goods, is doomed to bitter disappointment. It is a fair price set upon it, and he is not half a man who attempts to get it for less. They who 'cut across lots' to success reach failure first. An important condition is to keep the road; it is a straight and narrow way with here and there a traveller, a rough way often, hilly and rocky, yet it is the only prescribed, direct, appointed road to the coveted goal."

Bancroft considered it worth his while to spend twenty-six years on the "History of the United States"; Gibbon, to plod for twenty years on the "Decline and Fall of the Roman Empire."

Rousseau was willing to pay in labour for his literary style. "My manuscripts," he says, "blotted, scratched, interlined, and scarcely legible, attest the trouble they cost me. There is not one of them which I have not been obliged to transcribe four or five times before it went to press. Some of my periods I have turned or returned in my head for five or six nights before they were fit to be put to paper."

Isaac Newton, after spending long years on an intricate calculation, had his papers destroyed by his dog Diamond—and then cheerfully began to replace them. Carlyle, after he had lent the manuscript of the "French Revolution" to a friend whose careless servant used it to kindle the fire, calmly rewrote it. It was part of the price of their greatness. Would you have had the courage to pay it, in the place of either?

Have you longed for an education, seeing no means to procure it? Not lack of schools and teachers, nor want of books and friends; not the most despised rank or calling; not poverty nor ill health, nor deafness nor blindness; not hunger, cold, weariness, care, nor sickness of heart, have been able to keep determined men from acquiring a good education.

Have you no money to buy books? Think of Thurlow Weed, who, in order to study nights by the light of a camp fire in a sugar orchard, walked through the snow two miles, with pieces of rag carpet tied about his feet for shoes, to borrow a coveted book. Lincoln, when a boy, walked twenty miles and back to obtain a book he could not afford to buy.

The son of a coal merchant, too poor to buy books, borrowed and copied three folio volumes of precedents, and the whole of "Coke on Littleton"; he was the boy who, as Lord Eldon, sat on the woolsack for fifty years.

Another boy, whose only inheritance was poverty and hard work, but who had an unquenchable thirst for knowledge and a determination to get on in the world, braided straw to get money to buy books which his soul thirsted for; he was Horace Mann, the great common-school director of Massachusetts, whose statue stands by the side of that of Webster at the State capitol, and whose name ranks high in the Hall of Fame.

A glover's apprentice of Glasgow, who was too poor to afford even a candle or a fire, but studied by the light of the shop windows in the streets, and who when the shops were closed, climbed a lamp post, holding his book in one hand and clinging to the lamp post with the other—this poor boy, with less chance than almost any boy in America, became one of the most eminent scholars of Scotland.

Have you the stamina to go on with your studies when too poor to buy bread, appeasing the pangs of hunger by tying tighter and tighter about your body a girdle, as did Samuel Drew or John Kitto?

The "royal road to learning" is a myth. If you see no way open except a thorn-beset path, have you the stuff in you to follow it, turning neither to the right hand nor to the left?

Do you desire to be an orator and sway the minds of men? Would you train your voice for months on the seashore with only the waves for your audience, like Demosthenes? Would you, like him, cure yourself of a peculiar shrug by

practising with naked shoulders under the sharp
point of a suspended sword? Could you stand
calm and unmoved in Faneuil Hall, amid hisses
and showers of rotten eggs, like Wendell Phillips? Would you keep on your feet in parliament, like a Disraeli, when every sentence is
hailed with derisive laughter? Could you stand
your ground, as he did, until you had compelled
the applause of the critics? Have you the determination that carried Curran again and again to
speak in that august parliament where he had
been so often hissed? Would you, like Savon-
arola, Cobden, Sheridan, and scores of others who
broke down completely at their first attempts,
persevere in spite of repeated ignominious failures? If, like Daniel Webster, you were too
bashful and awkward as a schoolboy to declaim
in public, would you push on to become the most
popular orator in America?

A young man went to Chitty for advice about
studying law. "Can you eat sawdust without
butter?" was the great barrister's abrupt demand,
signifying that the mortification of the flesh in
the days of one's youth is the price of distinction.

Make up your mind, once for all, that he who
would succeed must pay. He must not look for
a "soft job." Into work which he feels to be a
part of his very existence he must pour his whole
heart and soul. He must be fired by a determina-

tion which knows no defeat, which cares not for hunger or ridicule, which spurns hardships and laughs at want and disaster. The men who have pushed the world up from chaos into the light of the highest civilisation, who, as they climbed, lifted others also to a higher plane, were not men of luck and broadcloth, nor of legacy and laziness. They were men inured to hardship and deprivation—not afraid of threadbare clothes and honest poverty, men who fought their way to their own loaf.

If you are built of such material as this, you will succeed; if not, in spite of all your dreams and wishes, you will fail.

CHAPTER X

RUSKIN'S MOTTO

"TO-DAY," inscribed upon a large piece of chalcedony, was the motto Ruskin kept upon his study table.

Time is exactly what we make it: In the hands of the wise, a blessing; in the hands of the foolish, a curse; in the hands of the wise, a preparation for life eternal; in the hands of the foolish, a preparation for self-condemnation and irreparable loss. What is it in your hands? Are you a time-server, or does time advance your work and increase your value as a worker? Show me a man who has benefited the world by his wisdom, or his country by his patriotism, or his neighbour by his philanthropy, and you show me a man who has made the best of every minute. The man who seizes the sixtieth part of an hour, as a miser seizes upon the smallest coin, will not waste the hour.

It has been calculated that the difference between rising at five and seven o'clock in the morning, for the space of forty years—supposing a man to go to bed at the same hour at night—is nearly equivalent to the addition of ten years to one's life. Dean Swift used to say that he never knew any man to come to eminence who lay in bed in the morning. Yet not a few eminent workers do their work in the night to secure freedom from interruption; like Alexander Graham Bell, the inventor of the telephone, who sleeps till noon, and works in the night.

Napoleon devoted only four hours to sleep; Lord Brougham spent the same time in bed, when he was the most celebrated man in England. Cobbett wrote: "What man ever performed a greater quantity of labour than I have performed? I have not, during my life, spent more than thirty-five minutes at table, including all the meals of the day." Bishop Burnett commenced his studies every morning at four o'clock; so did Bishop Jewell and Thomas Moore. Dr. Parkhurst, the philologist, rose at five. Gibbon was in his study every morning, winter and summer, at six o'clock. Guests at Abbotsford used to wonder when Scott found time to do his work, for he was always disengaged to entertain them. He had "broken the back of his work" while they were in their beds.

"To have any chance of success, I must be more studious than other men," Lord Campbell wrote to his father as an excuse for not visiting home; "I must be in chambers when they are at the theatre; I must study when they are asleep;

I must remain in town when they are in the country." A young man who sets out in life with such a spirit, knows the value of every moment in its relation to the work he wishes to achieve.

"For years I was in my place of business by sunrise," said a wealthy banker who had begun without a dollar, "and often I did not leave it for fifteen or eighteen hours."

"The industry of this Franklin," said Dr. Bard, "is superior to anything of the kind I have ever witnessed. I see him still at work when I return from the club at night, and he is at it again in the morning before the neighbours are out of bed."

Two young men were apprenticed to a carpenter and were very busy all day. One spent his evenings in study. The other often importuned him to "throw away those old books, and come out and have some fun," but he steadily declined, as the evenings were all too short for his study. Unknown to anyone but himself, he was fast becoming master of his business in its minutest details. One day there was an offer in the paper for the best plan of a state house, with a prize of two thousand dollars. The young carpenter determined to submit his ideas. He worked quietly, not caring to be joked about his failure to win. The plans were sent in, and he won the prize. While he had been studying, the other boy idled his time away, and he is still plodding on as a day labourer, hardly able to earn a living for his family.

If you want to know a young man's character, find out what he does with his spare minutes. What do they mean to him? What does he see in them? Does he see education, self-culture, a coveted book, in the odd moments and half-holidays which others throw away; or does he see a sparring match, a saloon, a gambling place, horse racing or a pool table?

In ingrained habits of hard work lies one great secret of success, the habit of systematically saving time, extracting from every minute its utmost possibility, making every "to-day" stand for something worthy of its immortal hours.

CHAPTER XI

THE TUNE OF THE ATOMS AND THE SONG OF THE BEES

For the world was built in order,
And the atoms march in tune.
                              EMERSON.

So work the honey-bees,
Creatures that by a rule in nature teach
The act of order to a peopled kingdom.
                              SHAKESPEARE.

LIVES modelled in conformity with the divine law of order gather to themselves, in large measure, the strength and harmony and beauty that run through all nature. They are working in unity with the Power that guides the planets in their courses and brings the seasons in their turn.

It has been said that the difference between a man of capacity and one of no capacity is, in the main, a question of method. The methodical man, by an orderly, systematic arrangement of his work, conserves the energy of mind and body that is frittered away unconsciously, and without adequate return by the unmethodical man. The former accomplishes far more than the latter within the same time, and with a sense of enjoyment in his labour unknown to the man who works without a plan.

The student who works at haphazard, devoting himself assiduously to his books for several hours to-day, trying to make up for the time lost yesterday, because he was not in the mood for study, or because he could not resist some social allurement, will never reach the front rank either in school or in life. Musicians declare that the pupil who practises regularly two hours a day will make far more rapid progress than the one who, filled with ardour one day, works six or eight hours, and does not apply himself again, perhaps, for two or three days. He may give more time in the aggregate to practise than the methodical pupil; but, because his efforts are spasmodic, without system, they are robbed of half their value. Even musical geniuses like Paderewski, great singers like Nordica and Sembrich, must practise daily in order to keep themselves " up to concert pitch." An operatic star once remarked to an intimate friend: " If I neglect practising one day I notice a falling off in my voice myself; if I do not practise for two days, my friends notice it; and if I fail to practise for three days my audience notices it."

So high a value did Ruskin place upon order and system that he rated them as " nobler things than power." Their influence in modelling successful lives can hardly be exaggerated. The men and women who have become distinguished in various walks of life owe more than half their success to the habit, cultivated in childhood, of arranging their work in such a way as to extract from every moment of time its utmost value. If parents would teach their children, from their earliest years, to be methodical and orderly in their habits, would insist that the well-worn maxims "A place for everything and everything in its place," and "A time for everything and everything in its time," are not mere parrot expressions, but basic principles of right living, there would be fewer failures to record. Disorder and confusion, lack of method or system, breed mental and moral discord, and a discontented, unhappy life results.

We often wonder how it is that some men, with mediocre ability, accomplish so much more than others with greater ability. Inquiry will show that the difference is due to the better application of time, and to methodical habits. A methodical man, with moderate ability, may, for instance, build up a great business, while a man with great ability, without the habit of system and order, can never get beyond a small business. No important establishment can be built up without rigid system and order. Men like John

Wanamaker, Marshall Field, Philip D. Armour, institute large establishments simply because they have genius for organisation and understand the might of method.

"All my life," said Armour, "I have been up with the sun. The habit is as easy at sixty-one as it was at sixteen. I have breakfast by half-past five or six. I walk down town to my office, and am there by seven, and I know what is going on in the world without having to wait for others to come and tell me. At noon, I have a simple luncheon of bread and milk, and, after that, usually, a short nap, which freshens me again for the afternoon's work. I am in bed again at nine o'clock every night."

Who shall estimate how large a part this systematic plan of living played in the success of the founder of the Armour Institute, one of Chicago's greatest schools.

"Everything in this establishment is run by system," said the managing inspector of one of America's largest stores; " it couldn't be run successfully in any other way. A great store is like a great army, and must be conducted just as carefully. A false step may mean a loss of thousands of dollars, just as a false move in battle may cause a great loss of life. Every move must be carefully planned in order to avoid mistakes. We employ about twenty-two hundred people.

Everyone knows his or her place, and things move as easily as if we had but twenty-two employees."

"Different affairs are arranged in my head," said Napoleon, "as in drawers. When I wish to interrupt one train of thought, I close the drawer which contains that subject, and open that which contains another. They do not mix together, and do not fatigue or inconvenience me. I have never been kept awake by an involuntary preoccupation of the mind. If I wish repose, I shut up all the drawers, and I am asleep. I have always slept when I wanted rest, and almost at will."

Success in any line of work or study, for the average man or woman, is dependent to a great extent on order and method.

Irregularity and want of method are only supportable in men and women of great learning or genius, who are often too full to be exact, and therefore choose to throw down their pearls in heaps before the reader or hearer rather than be at the pains of stringing them. But even genius without order, Buffon says, loses three-fourths of its power. "Genius alternates periods of frantic application with spells of idleness in which spent forces recover tone; but talent proceeds more steadily and smoothly. Its rests are regular and its work more methodical."

It was a matter of astonishment to Europe

that Luther, amid all his travels and active labours, could present a perfect translation of the Bible. But a single word explains it. He had a rigid system of doing something every day. " *Nulla dies*," says he in answer to the question how he accomplished so great an undertaking, " *Nulla dies sine versu* " (no day without a verse). Without an exact system it would have been impossible for him in addition to his labour in other lines, to have written seven hundred volumes during his life. John Wesley, who travelled and preached much of his time, yet found leisure to write thirty-two octavo volumes before his seventieth year. Longfellow, by working regularly a short time each morning, within a comparatively short time translated Dante's " Divine Comedy."

One of the most popular of our writers and orators was once asked how he managed to get through such a prodigious amount of work. " Simply by organising my time," he replied.

If Alfred the Great had not made himself famous as one of the best and wisest of England's kings, he would have been distinguished as a scholar and author. He became one of the most learned men of his age by so systematically arranging his time that no moment was without its appointed task. Historians tell us that he divided the twenty-four hours of the day into three equal portions; one of these he appropriated to public business and affairs of state; another to reading, study, and religious duties; and the third to bodily exercises, riding, hunting, various sports and recreations, repasts, and sleep. Clocks were not then invented, so he continued to measure time by means of six tapers of a certain length, which lasted four hours each, in lanterns, placed at the entrance of his palace, and his chaplain gave him notice when one of them was consumed.

Punctuality and method, it has been truly observed, are the right and the left hand of time. The man who possesses them is always on time. He enjoys his work because everything he does is systematic, orderly, complete. There is no hurry or confusion. He makes his plans and carries them out with perfect ease and regularity.

Method and order are not only conservers of energy, but they are the surest means to the attainment of a healthy, happy life. " Order," says Southey, "is the sanity of the mind, the health of the body, the peace of the city, the security of the state. As the beams to a house, as the bones to the body, so is order to all things."

Imprisoned within the icebergs of the Arctic region, with no prospect of release for months to come, Dr. Kane sustained the failing energies of the remnant of his crew, and, enfeebled though the men were by disease and privation, maintained discipline by adhering strictly to the regular

performance of the duties of each day. Of that
time he remarked: " It is the experience of every
man who has either combated difficulties himself or
attempted to guide others through them, that the
controlling law shall be systematic action. Nothing depresses and demoralises so much as a surrender of the approved and habitual forms of life.
I resolved that everything should go on as it had
done. The arrangement of hours, the distribu-
tion and details of duty, the religious exercises,
the ceremonials of the table, the fires, the lights,
the watch, the labours of the observatory, and the
notation of the tides and of the phenomena of the
sky—nothing should be intermitted that had contributed to make up the day."

Few things are more demoralising or disas-
trous to success than a habit of doing one's work
without method or order. When once allowed
to get a hold upon a young life, this habit is almost
sure to lead to unfortunate results. The boy or
girl who does his or her work anyhow, at any
time, who always throws things down wherever
they have been used, and leaves them lying about
in confusion, is starting on the road to failure.

No matter what you are, employer or employee,
in business or out of it, arrangement simplifies
the execution of anything that has to be done;
by it a business, no matter how large, will go on
as smoothly and regularly as a well-constructed

machine; without it, all is confusion and disorder. Successful men possess the great gift of methodical, well-balanced, arranging minds; they are men who cannot work in disorder, but will have things straight and know all the details, which enables them so to arrange the machinery of their affairs that they are fully cognisant alike of its strength, weakness, and capability, and they judiciously and discreetly exercise all its power to the uttermost.

"God is a God of order. Everything is arranged upon definite principles, and never at random." If we do not work with Him we work against Him; and a life without plan or system is contrary to all law and order.

CHAPTER XII

WRITING UPON THE ROCK

I T is better," said Gladstone, "to write one word upon the rock than a thousand on the water and sand."

It is better to know how to do one thing well than to have an imperfect knowledge of many things. God never intended that one man should be a doctor, a lawyer, a pianist, a carpenter, a machinist, a stenographer, and a dozen other things besides. The men who have risen to the highest places in life have kept close to a single line of effort.

"What you want, more than anything else, is to know how to do something well," said President McKinley addressing the pupils of an industrial school in Texas. "If you will just learn how to do one thing that is useful better than anybody else can do that one thing, you will never be out of a job." "If you make a good pin," it is remarked by a successful manufacturer, "you will earn more than if you make a bad steam engine." Who does not hate to see a thing done by halves? "If it be right, do it boldly; if it be wrong, leave it undone." .Whoever knew half-heartedness to win?

"Nearly half a century ago," said a railroad man, "I was put upon the world to make a living. I was stout and willing. I secured a place in a hardware store, to do odd jobs at seventy-five dollars a year. When I had been at work some three months, a customer bought a large bill of shovels, tongs, sad-irons, pans, buckets, scuttles, etc., for he was to be married the next day and was supplying his household in advance, as was then the custom. The articles were packed on a wheel-barrow, making a load heavy enough for a mule. But, more willing than able, I started off, proud that I could move such a mass, and got along finely until I reached the 'mud road' which is now Seventh Avenue. The wheel sank half its depth, and I could not budge the load. A good-natured Irishman, however, passing on a dray, took my barrow and its load on his vehicle and landed me at the house of the customer. I counted the articles carefully, as I delivered them, and then trudged back with the empty wheel-barrow, whistling with pleasure at my triumph. But my employers did not refund the piece of silver I had paid to the drayman. The next day, however, a merchant sent for me, and told me that he had witnessed my struggles and noted my zeal, especially the care with which I counted the pieces as I delivered my load. As a reward for my cheerful persistence under difficulty and my thoroughness, he offered me a five-hundred dollar clerkship. With the consent of my employers, I accepted, having literally wheeled myself into the road to fortune."

You may wonder why you are not advanced, or why someone else is promoted above you when you feel that you are more worthy. But are you really in line for promotion? Have you studied every detail of your business as an artist studies his canvas? Have you read books which bear upon your vocation, in order to broaden your knowledge and make you of more value to your employer in the event of your promotion? Are you the best man or woman in your department? If you cannot answer these questions in the affirmative—if you are not better qualified than anyone around you—then you cannot expect to be advanced.

Whatever you undertake, go to the bottom of it, and do not allow any employee to know more about your business than you do. Determine that you will master the subject, and be able to give points to everybody under you. The very reputation of being a master in your calling, of knowing it from A to Z will be of untold advantage to you, and may save you, not only from many embarrassments, but also from utter failure in some great panic or emergency. Nothing in the line of your effort is too trivial or small for your attention. Let this be your motto: "I will be master of whatever I undertake."

"How is it that you do so much?" asked one in astonishment at the efforts and success of a great man.

"Why, I do but one thing at a time, and try to finish it once for all."

In what other country is so much poor work done as in America? Did you never know half-trained masons and carpenters throw buildings together to sell, which sometimes fortunately fell in a wind storm before being occupied? Did you never know a half-trained medical student perform a bungling operation and put a patient to great risk because he was not willing to take time for thorough preparation? Did you never know a half-trained lawyer stumble through his case, and make his clients pay for experience which the schools should have given him? Did never a half-trained clergyman speak unadvisedly in the pulpit? If you are only half prepared for your work, can you blame society for your failure? What is more needed than the teaching of thoroughness? Nature works for centuries to perfect a rose or a fruit; but an American youth is ready to try a difficult case in court after a few months' desultory law reading, or to undertake a critical surgical operation, upon which a precious life depends, after listening to two or three courses of medical lectures.

When Louis XIV. of France came to the throne and found himself with an uncultivated mind in the midst of the accomplished society of the age, he bitterly reproached the guardians of his childhood because they had suffered him to grow up in such ignorance. " Was there not birch enough in the forests of Fontainebleau? " he exclaimed.

What a misfortune it is to grow up to manhood and womanhood, conscious of possessing superior native ability, yet unable to fill positions of honour and trust because of defective application during one's childhood! How many people have failed in life simply because they were not taught in youth to do things accurately, properly, carefully.

If a youth once forms a habit of half doing things, or doing them in a half-hearted, slovenly manner, never quite finishing anything he undertakes, never quite working out his problems and lessons, relying upon his skill and sharpness and deceit to get through or to deceive his teacher, he will find that these defects will mar his whole career. If he goes to college, he will be known there as the boy with unprepared lessons and poor recitations, who barely " skins " through his examinations and gets his diploma, perhaps, by special favour. If he goes into business, there are always defects in his transactions; he lacks system, order, thoroughness; is slovenly in his habits, and never quite knows how he stands. He is not of much importance in the community, for nobody has confidence in his methods or judgment. He is always blundering; he is a little late at the bank, and his notes are protested; he misses his engagements, and disappoints those with whom they were made. He never thinks it worth while to be exacting in little things. His books are inaccurate; his papers and letters are never filed; his desk is loaded with papers and letters and confusion reigns everywhere. Such a man is always a failure, and is demoralising to his associates. His example is infectious. Everyone who works for him catches the contagion; and, knowing that their employer is not exacting, accurate, careful, thorough, employees come to see things as their master does, and these defects and weaknesses are perpetuated in their own careers.

Many men and women with superior aptitude for teaching, have been unable to obtain good positions on account of habits based upon the imperfect work of their youth in primary or common school work. Not a day goes by but fresh instances arise to prove, in things little and great, that lack of thoroughness is, in the end, the falsest kind of economy.

That a man or woman who, knowingly, does a poor job when receiving pay for a good one, is as much a thief as if abstracting money from another's pocket-book, is a truth that does not appear to strike home in many cases. This carelessness, this disregard for the rights of others, grows out of the failure to recognise the law of human brotherhood; and also from a failure to understand clearly that the one who thus refuses to do his duty really hurts himself and shadows his own soul, in a way for which no money gained for the moment can at all compensate.

A young lady working on a paper once said she did not try to do very good work for her employers, because they " did not pay much." This doing poor work because it does not pay much is just what keeps thousands and thousands of young people from getting on in the world. Small pay is no excuse for doing slovenly work. The pay which one receives should have nothing to do with the quality of his work.

Character is a very great factor in success, and the personal impression you make on your employer will tell. If not, it will attract the attention of others.

A millionaire in New York told the writer that, when he was a boy, he let himself out by verbal contract for five years, at seven dollars and fifty cents a week, in a large dry goods store in New

York. At the end of three years, this young man had developed such skill in judging goods that another concern offered him three thousand dollars a year to go abroad as its buyer. He said that he did not mention this offer to his employers, nor even suggest the breaking of his agreement to work for seven and a half dollars a week, although verbal, until his time was up. Many people would say he was very foolish not to accept the offer mentioned, but the fact was that his firm, in which he ultimately became a partner, paid him ten thousand dollars a year at the expiration of his seven-and-a-half-dollar-a-week contract. They saw that he was giving them many times the amount of his salary, and in the end he was the gainer. Supposing he had said to himself, " They give me only seven and a half dollars a week, and I will earn only seven and a half dollars a week; I am not going to earn fifty dollars a week when I am getting only seven and a half!" This is what many boys would have said, and then they would have wondered why they were not advanced.

Young people should start out with the conviction that there is only one way to do anything, and that is, the best it can be done, regardless of remuneration.

It is not merely a question of cheating an employer; it is a question of cheating yourself, when you do poor work. The employer is not injured half as much as you are by half-done work. It may be a loss of a few dollars to him, but to you it is loss of character and self-respect, loss of manhood or womanhood. These are woven from the warp and woof of daily work and thought. No one can afford to weave rotten or sleazy threads into the fabric of life.

"There are women," said Fields, "whose stitches always come out, and the buttons they sew on fly off at the mildest provocation; there are other women who use the same needle and thread, and you may tug away at their work on your coat, or waistcoat, and you can't start a button in a generation."

"These buttonholes, Sally," said Benjamin Franklin to his daughter, "are good for nothing. They will not wear. If you make a buttonhole, child, make the best buttonhole possible."

Not content with rebuking her, he went down the street and sent up a tailor, who had orders to instruct Miss Sarah in the art of making a buttonhole properly.

A great-granddaughter of the American philosopher told this anecdote recently, adding, with pride, "Since then the Franklin family have made buttonholes that will last."

Gladstone's children were taught to perform to the very end whatever they might begin, no matter how insignificant the undertaking might be.

Michael Faraday was coming out of a lecture room, one evening, after the lights were out, when he dropped something he carried in his hand. As he was groping about in the dark for it, a student remarked, "Never mind, if you don't find it to-night, to-morrow will do as well, I suppose." "That is true," said Faraday, "but it is of the gravest consequence to me, as a principle, that I be not foiled in my determination to find it."

"Either never attempt, or else accomplish," was the motto of the Duke of Dorset.

Francis Wayland used to tell of a student who kept school in vacation, and kept a very poor one. His excuse was that he intended not to be a schoolmaster, but a lawyer. The poor schoolmaster made a very poor lawyer.

When he was a young lawyer, Daniel Webster once looked in vain through all the law libraries near him, and then ordered at an expense of fifty dollars the necessary books, to obtain authorities and precedents in a case in which his client was a poor blacksmith. He won his cause, but, on account of the poverty of his client, charged only fifteen dollars, thus losing heavily on the books bought, to say nothing of his time. Years afterwards, as he was passing through New York City, he was consulted by Aaron Burr on an important and puzzling case then pending before the supreme court. He saw in a moment that it was just like the blacksmith's case, an intricate question of title, which he had solved so thoroughly that it was to him as simple as the multiplication table. Going back to the time of Charles II., he gave the law and precedents involved with such readiness and accuracy of sequence that Burr asked, in great surprise, if he had been consulted before in the case. "Certainly not," he replied, "I never heard of your case till this evening." "Very well," said Burr, "proceed;" and, when he had finished, Webster received a fee that paid him liberally for all the time and trouble he had spent for his early client. But it was not alone in the fee that he received his reward. He stood higher in his profession for the thoroughness of his work.

An eminent English lawyer studied years to gain a position at the bar. He had little success. He rode several circuits without a brief. At length, a friend gave him a case, because it was hopeless. An immense amount of property was involved in the suit. The whole case depended on the date of the establishment of a borough, which could not be found. The young lawyer went to work as if his life depended upon winning. He remembered that it was the custom of Sir Christopher Wren to place the date of his churches on the keystone. This borough had in it one of Wren's churches. All efforts to discover the date had been in vain. The young counsellor, having a strong impression that the date must be behind the inscription of the commandments and the creed, persuaded the sexton, worked nights, chipped away the plaster, and found the date. He won the case, and in time worked his way up to the woolsack. He used to say humorously that his success began with the breaking of all the commandments on one night.

The great French surgeon, M. Bourdon, was sent for one day to perform a critical operation upon Cardinal Du Bois, the prime minister under the old monarchy. "You must not expect, sir," remarked the cardinal upon the surgeon's entrance, "to treat me in the same rough manner in which you treat the poor miserable wretches at your hospital of the Hotel Dieu." "My lord," replied Bourdon, proudly, "every one of those miserable wretches, as your Eminence is pleased to call them, is a prime minister in my eyes."

The demand for perfection in the nature of Wendell Phillips was wonderful. Every word must exactly express the shade of his thought; every phrase must be of due length and cadence; every sentence must be perfectly balanced, before it left his lips. He was easily the first forensic

orator America has produced. The rhythmical
fullness and poise of his periods are remarkable.

"Where on earth," Jeffrey once asked Macaulay, "did you pick up that English style?"

"When a boy," said Macaulay, "I began to
read very earnestly, but at the foot of every page
I stopped, and obliged myself to give an account
of what I had read on that page. At first I had
to read it three or four times before I got my
mind firmly fixed; but now, after I have read a
book through once, I can almost recite it from beginning to end." He also said that he heard only
good English spoken, when a boy, and took
great pains to imitate it. He owed much, too,
to the advice of his mother, who once wrote to
him:

"I am very happy to hear that you have so far
advanced in your different prize exercises, and
with such little fatigue. I know you write with
great ease to yourself, and would rather write
ten poems than prune one; but remember that
excellence is not attained at first. All your
pieces are much mended after a little reflection;
take, therefore, some solitary walks and think
over each separate thing. Spare no time or
trouble to render each piece as perfect as you
can, and then leave the event without one anxious
thought. I have always admired a saying of one
of the old heathen philosophers. When a friend

was condoling with him that he so well deserved of the gods, and yet that they did not shower their favours on him, as on some others less worthy, he answered, 'I will, however, continue to deserve well of them.' So do you, my dearest."

Even Sheridan, who is commonly regarded as one of those marvellous geniuses who never open their mouths without dropping pearls of wit and wisdom, took good care to make a careful preparation, a close study of his subject, whenever any great effort was to be made. When the world gave him credit for being asleep, he was sitting up in his bed, early in the morning, preparing his witty sayings for the evening. It is known that he wrote and re-wrote, over and over again, several if not all of his brilliant comedies; hence their rare polish and abundance of sparkling wit.

There is hardly a bar in Beethoven's music of which it may not be said with confidence that it has been re-written a dozen times. Of the air, "O Hoffnung," in "Fidelio," the sketch-books show eighteen attempts, and of the concluding chorus, ten. Of many of the brightest gems of the opera, says Thayer, the first ideas are so trivial that it would be impossible to admit that they were Beethoven's if they were not in his own handwriting. And so it is with all his works. His favourite maxim was: "The barriers are not erected which can say to aspiring talent and industry, 'Thus far, and no farther.'"

Twenty things half done do not make one well done. Work which is not finished is merely a botch, an abortion. All the great masters have been workers who have really mastered their work.

"How did you attain such excellence in your profession?" was asked of Sir Joshua Reynolds. "By observing one simple rule," he replied; "namely, to make each picture the best."

When asked how he accomplished such wonders, Raphael replied, "From my earliest childhood I have made it a principle never to neglect anything."

Michael Angelo made every tool he used in sculpture, such as files, chisels, and pincers. In painting, he prepared all his own colours, and would not allow servants or students to mix them. From beginning to end, he performed the whole of his own work. Taking the marble as it came from the quarry, seldom making a model beyond a wax one, he immediately set to work with chisel and mallet on the figure, which was already perfected in his imagination. A French writer says of him: "I can say that I have seen him, when he was about sixty years of age, and not then very robust, make the fragments of marble fly about at such a rate that he cut off more in a quarter of an hour than three strong young men could have done in an hour—a thing almost incredible to anyone who had not seen it; and he used to work with such fury, with such an impetus, that it was feared he would dash the whole marble to pieces, making at each stroke chips of three or four fingers' thickness fly off;" with a material in which, if he had gone only a hair's breadth too far, he would have totally destroyed the work, which could not be restored like plaster or clay. He could trust his own hands. He knew that what he did himself was well done.

Every difficult exploit and every successful man is an object lesson in the science of success. The study of these lessons emphasises the fact, over and over again, that brilliant and uncommon endowments are not necessary for great achievements. Distinguished men and distinguished deeds usually depend upon very old-fashioned and homely virtues. One thing always prominent in the record is thoroughness.

" The situation that has not its duty, its ideals," says Carlyle, " was never yet occupied by man. Yes, here, in this poor, miserable, hampered, despicable actual, wherein thou even now standest, here or nowhere is thy ideal; work it out therefrom, and, working, believe, live, be free. The ideal is in thyself."

"Tack it on, Jimmy, the clobber'll hide it," said a horseshoer as he shambled out of his shop, leaving his step-son to shoe a pony. The boy looked after his step-father, then at the ill-fitting shoe he was told to put on the horse, depending on the mud of the road to hide its defects. He shook his head sadly. Then a determined look came over his face. "I'll not tack it on the way it is. It'll be a shoe, and a good one, before it goes on." He went over to the fire, and, when he was through with the bellows and the anvil, the shoe was perfectly fitted to the foot.

Yet it always puzzled Billy Farrell, the horseshoer below the bridge, who had all the soldiers' horses from the barracks, why John Shea, "the shiftless botch, the poorest mechanic in all Ireland," could "keep the shoein' o' Lady Forbes's pony." He did not know of the little step-son who was working out his ideal.

A lady once crossed a street where a small boy was busily sweeping the crossing. She noticed with pleasure the care with which he did his work, and smiled as she said to him:

"Yours is the cleanest crossing I pass."

He lifted his cap with a gallant air, and quickly said, "I am doing my best."

All day the words rang in her ears, and for many days afterwards, and, when a friend, a rich, influential man, inquired for a boy to do errands and general work for him, she told him of the little fellow at the crossing.

"A boy who would do his best at a street crossing is worth a trial with me," said the man; and he found the boy, engaged him for a month, and, at the end of that time, was so pleased with him that he sent him to school and fitted him for a position which he filled with honour.

"Doing my best at the street crossing made a successful man of me," he often said in after years.

"I tell you what, Billy Gray," exclaimed a mechanic, when reprimanded for slovenly work by a merchant prince of Boston: "I sha'n't stand such words from you. Why, I can remember when you were nothing but a drummer in a regiment!" "And so I was," replied Mr. Gray, "so I was a drummer; but didn't I drum well, eh?— didn't I drum well?"

When Andrew Johnson, in a celebrated speech at Washington, said that he had begun his political career as an alderman, and had held office through all the branches of the legislature, a man in the audience shouted, "From a tailor up." "Some gentleman says I have been a tailor," said the President; "that does not disconcert me in the least; for, when I was a tailor, I had the reputation of being a good one, and making close fits. I was always punctual with my customers, and always did good work."

It is no disgrace to be a shoemaker, but it is a disgrace for a shoemaker to make bad shoes.

"Labour," said William Ellery Channing, "may be so performed as to be a high impulse to the mind. Be a man's vocation what it may, his rule should be to do its duties perfectly, to do the best he can, and thus to make perpetual progress in his art. In other words, perfection should be proposed; and this I urge not only for its usefulness to society, nor for the sincere pleasure which a man takes in seeing a work well done. This is an important means of self-culture. In this way the idea of perfection takes root in the mind, and spreads far beyond the man's trade. He gets a tendency toward completeness in whatever he undertakes. Slack, slovenly performance in any department of life is more apt to offend him. His standard of action rises, and everything is better done for his thoroughness in his common vocation."

Many years ago, a college student was appointed to survey a tract of land in Western Nova Scotia. It was a barren region, covered mainly with granite boulders, and impassable except on foot. There was little fertile soil or valuable timber. The whole tract seemed not worth the cost of even a rough survey; and there seemed little prospect that any test would ever come to the work which this student might do. But the young man was true to his profession, and equally true to the idea that he must do his best. It is said that, even ten years ago, in the whole area of this survey of thirteen hundred and fifty square miles, there were only twenty-six residents. Since then, gold has been discovered in that rough territory, the "leads" being such that the successful finding of the gold depends upon the accuracy of the surveyor's calculations. Experts have followed in the path of that young student, seeking by trial and re-trial to locate the veins of gold. After their most careful work has been done, the government's best surveyors declare that their work was unnecessary, and that every one of the lines laid down by that college student have been proven as true as human knowledge can make them.

Do you ask what has been the life of this young man since he thus carefully surveyed the barren land of Nova Scotia? He is Sir William Dawson, and is now filling out a grand life at McGill University, Montreal.

The artisan is he who strives to get through his work—the artist, he who strives to perfect it.

"This is the culture of the imagination," said James Freeman Clark: "first, to learn to see the beauty and grace which God has poured out on sky, on land, and sea; on body and soul; on life and conduct; on society and art; then to be a creator of beauty as God creates it, carrying this idea of the perfect into all that we do, learning continually to think more exactly, speak more accurately, live more truly, and finish well all we undertake."

"Doing well depends upon doing completely," says the Persian proverb. Taking time and taking pains go a long way toward establishing the value of one's work. Craving for perfection goes far toward the making of a master workman. It is due to one's self, as well as to one's employer, to perform the duties of his position faithfully, efficiently, to the very best of his ability. The world wants no careless, indifferent, or half-hearted workers. It wants the best, and the slip-shod, don't-care, happy-go-lucky young man or woman will be tolerated only until a more competent person appears. The world expects, society demands, and my highest self calls upon me to do my best. I should feel that the universe is not quite complete without my work well done.

George Eliot expresses this thought finely in her poem, "Stradivarius," about the famous old violin-maker, whose violins, some of them about two hundred years old, are now worth from five to ten thousand dollars, or several times their weight in gold. She makes Stradivarius say:

"If my hand slacked,
I should rob God—since he is fullest good—
Leaving a blank instead of violins.
He could not make Antonio Stradivari's violins
Without Antonio."

Make it a rule of your life, under all circumstances, to do whatever is given you to do, carefully, conscientiously, thoroughly, be it ever so trifling; for he only who is painstaking in small things will be entrusted with larger responsibilities. To do your best; to put your whole heart into your work; to fill your place as it never was filled before; to make yourself abundantly worthy of better things; this is to follow the path that leads to great achievements. Only by doing your best in the position you now occupy will you ever attain to anything better. Powers and capabilities develop by use, and, if you are content to do but half your best, you are as surely burying your talent as if you put it into the ground. Don't worry or fret because you think you are capable of doing a higher class of work than that in which you are now engaged. If you have great qualities in you, they will find their way to the surface, no matter how humble your position.

" Seest thou a man diligent in his business? He shall stand before kings." Be faithful and diligent in performing the duties of to-day, and to-morrow the larger opportunity will come and find you ready.   There is only one means to success in life—honest, painstaking labour. There is no other way to build up a noble character, to attain to the highest manhood or womanhood. Make up your mind at the outset that you will be your own most rigid taskmaster; that, even in the smallest things, you will accept nothing but your best, and your life will grow broader, richer, and more useful day by day.

" The first great work is that yourself may to yourself be true," and only by constantly putting forth your highest powers, by always being and doing your best, can you accomplish this supreme end.

CHAPTER XIII

THE MAN OF FORCE

S HOW me," said Caliph Omar to the warrior Amru, "that sword with which you have fought so many battles and slain so many infidels." "Ah," replied Amru, "the sword without the arm of the master is no sharper nor heavier than the sword of Farezdak the poet." One hundred and fifty pounds of human flesh and blood weigh nothing in the scale of manhood without weight of will and tenacity of purpose.

"There is always room for a man of force," said Emerson. The world is always demanding men who can make an intelligent and independent use of their will power. Original force, constructive energy, is always at a premium. The thinker, the man of original ideas and methods of productive power, who can start out in untrodden paths and open the way for others—this is the man much to be sought for.

Many men fail to get on in the world because of their lack of mental energy. Their minds seem incapable of independent action. If some one would give them a push, and set them going, they might continue to move; but they cannot start—they have no self-momentum. Many of these people are set aside all along the road of life, not because of their incapacity, but because the fatal lack of mental energy seems to have paralysed their faculties. They possess power, but are apparently helpless to use it.

The great achievers, the men who do something in the world, are men of strong mentality. If they do not possess a robust physique, they have tremendous vigour and will power which enable them not only to plan great enterprises, but also to overcome all obstacles in carrying them to a successful issue. There is nothing uncertain, nothing negative in the make-up of the man of force. He is positive to the backbone. He does not need bolstering up; he can stand alone.

It is not so much what he says that impresses you with his strength as what he does not say; his very silence carries power. You feel that there is a large reserve back of everything he says or does.

General Grant said very little, but no one could be with him five minutes without feeling that he was in the presence of a great character. Webster did not impress his hearers half so much by what he said as by the feeling he inspired of the mighty reserve he could marshal to the front in case of necessity.

Learning that Napoleon would soon pass along through a long, dim passage, a young man hid there, that he might slay the ruthless invader of his country. As the Emperor approached, his massive head bowed in thought, the young man raised his weapon, took careful aim, and was about to press the trigger when a slight noise betrayed his presence. Napoleon looked up and comprehended the situation at a glance. He did not speak, but gazed intently upon the youth, a smile of haughty challenge upon his face. The weapon fell from nerveless hands, and the hero of a hundred battles passed on in silence, his head again bowed in meditation upon affairs of state. To him it was but one incident in a crowded career, a mere personal triumph soon lost sight of amid memories of battles which shook the world with the thunder of his victorious legions. To the young man it was the experience of a lifetime, a crushing, bewildering sense of his own inferiority in comparison with the weight of character of the man who threw a measureless power into the life he was living. As well might the glow-worm match himself against the lightning!

"O Iole, how didst thou know that Hercules was a god?" "Because," answered Iole, "I was content the moment my eyes fell on him. When I beheld Theseus, I desired that I might see him offer battle, or at least drive his horses in the chariot race; but Hercules did not wait for a contest; he conquered whether he stood, or walked, or sat, or whatever else he did."

There are men and women in every country who conquer before they speak, and who exert an influence out of all proportion to their ability; and people wonder what is the secret of their power over men. The largest part of their power is latent. What others effect by talent or eloquence, the man of character accomplishes by a magnetic presence. "Half his strength he puts not forth." His victories are by demonstration of superiority, and not by crossing bayonets. He conquers because his arrival alters the face of affairs.

In 1794 the Royalists and Jacobins rose against the young republic of France—forty thousand men under determined veteran generals, opposed to five thousand under the mild, inefficient General Menou. The latter retired, and insurgent shouts of victory resounded through the streets of Paris. Night fell upon a scene of tumult, and at eleven o'clock the doom of the republican convention seemed sealed. In utmost alarm, Menou was deposed and Barras was given supreme command. "I know the man who can defend us, if anyone can," said Barras, hesitating to assume the proffered responsibility. "It is a young Corsican officer, Napoleon Bonaparte, whose military abilities I witnessed at Toulon.

He is a man that will not stand upon ceremony."
To the surprise of the convention, he then introduced "a small, slender, pale-faced, smooth-
cheeked young man, apparently about eighteen
years of age."

"Are you willing to undertake the defence of
the convention?" asked the president.

"Yes," replied Napoleon laconically.

"Are you aware of the magnitude of the
undertaking?"

"Perfectly; and I am in the habit of accom-
plishing that which I undertake. But one condition is indispensable. I must have the unlimited
command, entirely untrammelled by any orders
from the convention."

The vote giving him full command seemed instantaneously to transform the diminutive, statue-
like soldier into a man of more than mortal mould,
lightning-like in thought and plan, resistless in
will, electric in action. All night he toiled with
almost superhuman energy, and the most phleg-
matic soldier seemed to have caught the spirit
of his chief. Eight hundred muskets, with cartridges in abundance, were taken to the Tuileries,
where the convention was in session, and the
members were made a reserve corps. Streets
were barricaded, and cannon loaded with grape-
shot to the muzzle were posted so as to sweep
every bridge and avenue by which a hostile force

could approach his little army. The clangour of alarm bells and the passionate throb of drums greeted the dawn. With exultant music and flaunting banners, the insurgents moved to the attack. Seeing that Napoleon and his men stood firm, the advance columns leveled their muskets and fired. "It was the signal for an instantaneous discharge," says J. S. C. Abbott, "direct, sanguinary, merciless, from every battery. In quick succession, explosion followed explosion and a perfect storm of grape-shot swept the thronged streets. The pavements were covered with the mangled and the dead. The columns wavered— the storm still continued; they turned—the storm still raged unabated; they fled in utter dismay in every direction—the storm still pursued them. Then Napoleon commanded his little division impetuously to follow the fugitives, and to continue to discharge, but with blank cartridges. As the thunder of those heavy guns reverberated along the streets, the insurgents dispersed through every available lane and alley, and in less than an hour the foe was nowhere to be found." He disarmed the inhabitants, buried the dead and carried the wounded to the hospitals, and then, " with his pale and marble brow as unmoved as if no event of any great importance had occurred, returned to his headquarters at the Tuileries." After years of unparalleled disorder and blood-

shed, the capital had at length found its master:
"This is my seal," he said grimly, "which I
have impressed upon Paris."

It was the seal of an iron decision, and all
recognised it at sight.

Whether the man who does not "come forth
with purpose in his eye," and able to say "I am
resolved what to do" is fit to win or not, in the
great majority of cases he will not win. Decision
as to one's course is like the foundation of a
house. If this foundation is weak and apt to
give way, or is made of too slight material to
bear the required weight without being crushed,
it is, wholly or in some degree, useless if not
dangerous. So a half-decision on which one may
act for a time, only to have it topple or crumble,
is a waster of time and money, and a weakness of
character. One's indecision and vacillation seldom affect himself alone. One life so touches,
directly or indirectly, thousands of other lives,
that its weakness or its strength becomes, in some
degree, the weakness or the strength of all those
lives.

The secret of Joan of Arc's success was that
she saw the problem, and determined to solve it.
Not in her courage nor her visions, but in her
decision, or the rare qualities which go to make
up decision, was her strength. She pronounced
Charles VII. the heir, in God's name; reassured

him of his legitimacy, and sanctified this declaration by gaining a victory over the English.

" When I have once taken a resolution," said Cardinal Richelieu, " I go straight to my aim; I overthrow all, I cut down all."

Prompt decision and sublime audacity have carried many a successful man over perilous crises, where deliberation would have been ruin.

When the preliminary survey was being made for the railroad line between St. Petersburg and Moscow, Nicholas learned that the officers intrusted with the task were being influenced more by personal than by technical considerations and he determined to cut the Gordian knot in true imperial style. When the minister laid before him the map, with the intention of explaining the proposed route, he took a ruler, drew a straight line from one terminus to the other, and remarked, in a tone that precluded all discussion, " You will construct the line so." The line was thus constructed.

Count Von Moltke, the great German strategist and general, chose for his motto, " First weigh, then venture," and it is to this he owed his great victories and successes. He was slow, cautious, careful in planning, but bold, daring, even seemingly reckless in execution the moment his resolve was made.

The man who decides, whether a general,

statesman, or artist, says: "I have grasped the situation, taken the hilltop, obtained a comprehensive view; the only thing now, and from now on, is to act. The discussion is closed. The council of war is dismissed. Generals, to your divisions. The will now takes its regnant place. Decision is in the saddle, leading the hosts."

"They are harmless enough, perhaps," says a strong writer, in speaking of people who are forever hesitating between two, or more, opinions; "they have no personality, no colour, no self-reliance, no incisive vigour. They are perfectly commonplace, the train-bearers in the procession of life; the lay figures of the world, of whom the portrait of one would serve for that of a thousand; ciphers of humanity, who need some true man to stand before them to give them value; neuters in the hive, whose worth is only negative; human clay, for others to knead, and bake, and build into fortunes. They don't know what manly strength of character means; they pass and repass like shadows, and almost beg pardon for being alive; sandwich their sentences with apologies, as if people cared for such trumpery; are overtaken by events while still irresolute; and let the tide ebb before they push weakly off. They never know their own minds, but, like Coleridge, debate with themselves, the whole journey, which side of the road they will take, and, meanwhile,

keep winding from one to the other, in their di-
lemma. Or they stop at each flower, and turn up
each lane, instead of keeping ahead. Self-respect
lies at the bottom of manly decision; a just and
dignified self-esteem, which does not abase itself
meanly before either things or men. Greed, also,
has something to do with the want of it, for the
ass between the two bundles of hay clearly fell a
victim to the wish to have only the best, and
there are a great many long-eared brethren, heirs
of his troubles. Modesty is becoming, but it does
not require you to have no opinion or choice, or
to follow first one and then another by turns, like
a lost dog. The weakness that cannot decide,
for fear of making a bad bargain, is costly in
every sense. Firmness and decision, after due
thought and inquiry, are inseparable from any
conception of manliness. It is grand to be self-
complete; to hear opinions, it may be, but to judge
and act for one's self. Quick penetration and intelligence, comprehension, the viewing of facts together, comparison—the mental power to set
things side by side and perceive the greater, the
wiser, the more effective of different plans or
powers—sagacity, foresight of probable results—these seem to be the intellectual qualities
which go with or precede those decisions which
have secured success. Knowledge should come
first; then, decision of action. "To know a thing

is right and not to do it, is weakness," says Confucius. "Be sure you are right, then go ahead," are the familiar words of a famous American character. The power to conclude belongs to decision; it is, in fact, in the last analysis—the decision itself. *Con* and *claudo,* say the etymologists, mean to close together, to stop, as you shut the gates of a lock of a canal. The bank is closed—that is the end of the day's business. Success in life depends very largely upon our skill in knowing what not to do. Time-wasters are as thick as bees all about us; and, unless we set our faces like a flint toward those things which are absolutely indispensable to success, and sacrifice all the little trifles which destroy precious moments, we shall accomplish nothing worthy of a great life. Weak-minded youths, who allow themselves to be pulled hither and thither by the strongest influence which happens to be acting at the moment, who have not the incisive resolution to choose and stick to one unwavering aim, may do something, but they will never fulfill their mission, nor perform any work worthy of the gift of life and its opportunities. Trying to accomplish any appreciable results with a divided mind and unfocused energy, is like endeavouring to move an engine whose boiler is full of pin holes, each of which is letting out steam."

The world is full of unfortunates languishing

in prisons, suffering tortures in houses of infamy, dying in poorhouses, in miserable cellars and attics, because of weak minds which have been imposed upon, absorbed and used by stronger ones. It is ever the survival of the fittest. The stronger use the weaker, and the unfit become extinct. Half of the misery and suffering in the world come from weakness of mind and lack of decision. No matter what a person's capabilities may be, no matter what he promises to become; if he lacks decision, he is ever at the mercy of circumstances, and the puppet of stronger minds. The habit of decision is more important than anything else in early life. The world is full of failures who could not say " No!" with emphasis. One decided " No," spoken at the right moment, with energy, would have saved many a life from becoming a total wreck.

The will is the great driving wheel of the mental engine.

How many strong intellects suffer the humiliation of seeing one-talented men, but with great power of decision, forging far ahead in the race of life, while they, with ponderous intellects and colossal abilities, flounder about, creating great expectations, only to disappoint, simply because they lack the power of resolving vigorously.

There is nothing else which will fix a floating life, and prevent it from being tossed hither and thither, like forming a habit of prompt decision, and thus putting one's self forever beyond the temptation of vacillation from the influence of others. The will being the king of the intellectual kingdom, anarchy must reign when the leader is demoralised. Every youth should early learn that, both in business and morals, " He who hesitates is lost."

Someone has said that " the worst vice is advice." Certain it is that the " soul's emphasis," if the soul can think and feel intelligently, is, speaking broadly, "always right," and that one can far more easily decide matters for himself than anyone can decide them for him. To decide profitably for another, one should see from that other's standpoint, have that other's environments, capabilities, limitations, aspirations and preferences. This being impossible, to make a wise decision for him is equally impossible. There are thousands of lives and careers ruined or hindered, every year, because certain persons ask advice and those who are asked give it. This, of course, does not mean that one never should take counsel with another, but it is never safe or profitable to wait to talk things over with many people, or to allow one's sober, intelligent judgment to be overruled by another.

An educated will must be self-reliant, self-restrained, self-directed, and under self-control.

Sometimes a person finds himself in an emergency where he must make an immediate decision, although aware that it is not a matured decision approved by the whole cabinet of his mental powers. In that case he must bring all his comprehension and comparison into active, instant exercise, and feel that he is making the best decision he knows how at the time, and act. Many important decisions of life are of this kind, made off-hand.

There is nothing which will help a vacillating mind like forming a habit of always acting promptly and energetically. One should then never allow the contemplative or reflective faculties continually to bring up first one side and then the other, balancing motives, and splitting hairs over non-essentials. The decision would better be final and irrevocable, and carried out with energy, even if sometimes wrong, than that one should form a habit of forever balancing, contemplating, and procrastinating. After this habit of prompt decision has been cultivated, even mechanically for a time, confidence in one's judgment will begin to produce a new spirit of independence.

It is the decided man, the man of quick, prompt, and firm decision, who has the confidence of his fellow men, and who is usually placed in positions of trust. Nobody wants to see the vacillating, irresolute character in a responsible position.

A story is told of the nomination, a few years ago, of a governor of the State of New York. "A popular candidate of brilliant talents was considered favourably by the party leaders who were to make the nomination. They met him at dinner, the night before the caucus. He had finical tastes and hesitated anxiously over every dish.

" 'Game, sir?' asked the waiter, at length.

" 'What have you? Ah, quail! Bring me quail—or, no! Here is pheasant. A bit of pheasant, if you please.'

" While the man was gone, he was silent and anxious, and, when the pheasant appeared, he whispered, ' I think I'll try both. A quail, please. Yes, a little of both.' But, when both plates were set before him, he shoved them aside with disgust, exclaiming, ' Take them away! I won't have any game at all.'

" When the dinner was over and he had left the room, an almost unanimous expression of opinion passed around the table.

" 'No, gentlemen,' said the leader, ' the man who is so irresolute that he cannot decide what meat to eat, lacks an essential quality that is needed in the governor of the State of New York.'

" The nomination was given to a man who, as governor, and afterwards as president, whatever his shortcomings, was never accused of irresolution or of unnecessary delay in making up his mind."

"A man without decision," says John Foster, "can never be said to belong to himself; since, if he should dare to assert that he did, the puny force of some cause might make a seizure of the unhappy boaster the very next minute, and contemptuously exhibit the futility of the determination by which he was to have proved the independence of his understanding and will. He belongs to whatever can make capture of him; and one thing after another vindicates its right by arresting him while he is trying to go on, as twigs floating near the edge of a river are intercepted by every weed and whirled in every little eddy."

"To educate one's self up to a just decision of character, is part of that moral and mental training which constitutes the chief work of life, by which alone one can attain to 'the stature of the perfect man.'"

CHAPTER XIV

A MASTER PASSION

W HAT is your friend, young Tomp-kins?" one man asked of another. "A tramp," was the reply. "A tramp!" exclaimed the first speaker. "Surely you don't mean that he goes on the road!" "Oh, no," was the answer. "He's a thought-tramp. He is, he believes, capable of doing a number of things, and he cannot, or will not, determine which of these things he will adopt as a life work. He sometimes dips into one thing for a day, a week, or a month, and then leaves it for something else, which, in turn, is abandoned for a third thing, and so on. Oftener he is altogether idle, because he does not force himself to fix upon something as a steady pursuit. He is called brilliant and versatile, and I'm afraid his brilliancy and ver-satility will ruin him. If he had only one talent, or the power of making up his mind and sticking to his decision, I should have large hopes of him."

A certain man was graduated with honours from Harvard. He was handsome, agreeable, magnetic, full of vigour and vitality. He tried for success in the lecture field, but soon abandoned that for editorial work, which was soon replaced by a teachership. He became superintendent of schools in one place, took charge of the advertising department of a publication in another, opened a school of his own in a third, experimented in mining in a fourth, and so on. He travelled thousands of miles, while engaged in these different pursuits, spending many hundreds of dollars. After passing twelve years in this way, he had no settled pursuit, no sure position or salary, and was often hard pushed to pay his weekly bills.

"If you say to yourself," says President Jordan, "I will be a naturalist, or a traveller, or an historian, or a statesman, or a scholar; if you never unsay it; if you bend all your powers in that direction, and take advantage of all those aids that help toward your ends, and reject all that do not, you will some time reach your goal. The world turns aside to let any man pass who knows whither he is going. Your predestined place will wait your coming. Take time enough to reach it. Patient years must be yours, to make ready. Take time enough."

In choosing a profession, how many young men sit down and carefully examine their own capabilities, make a decision, and then with unremitting persistency bend every energy to the accomplishment of their purpose? Where one does this, perhaps ten slip, or slide, or stumble into the occupation that is nearest, easiest, and most convenient, thinking only of immediate pleasure or necessity, and with no well-defined plans for the future. Most people do not make a deliberate choice of the society in which they mingle, but fall into whatever comes along, and are as well satisfied as they would be in any other company. The average voters scamper here and there in flocks after some purposeful man, like sheep that follow a bell-wether. It is an occurrence much more infrequent than it ought to be for a young person entering upon an active career to sit down and thoughtfully consider the relation of the life that now is to the life that is to come, and then form a purpose to invest every moment of time in such a way that it will make for him the largest possible return in time and eternity.

Men drift into business. They drift into society. They drift into politics. They drift into what they fondly but vainly imagine is religion. If winds and tides are favourable, all is well; if not— and in this world they never are so always— all is wrong.

" Most men merely drift through life, and the work they do is determined by a hundred different circumstances," says Stalker. " They might as well be doing anything else, or they would prefer, if they could afford it, to be doing nothing at all."

"Youth to-day" says Ellis, "needs to hear a ringing prophet message, crying, 'Beware of crowds!' Half the evils that curse young womanhood and manhood are the consequence of doing as the crowd does. The spirit which gets its code of conduct from what 'everybody does' is most pernicious, and opposed to all true nobility and growth. Go with the multitude, and you will go nowhere worth the going. Follow the crowd, and you will be led astray. Drift with the common current, and you will drift into danger, defeat, and death."

The crying need of the present age is not for weather-vanes, always being flopped about with every gust of popular opinion. The demand, and it is an urgent one, is for men, high-minded men, stanch-hearted men, that dare to stand for the right and work with a purpose unmoved by popular clamour.

How often do we see persons with commanding abilities, with grand characters apparently, but who are always disappointing our expectations of their great promise. Magnificently educated and apparently well equipped for life's great work, they are like a chronometer which lacks only a little screw or a slender hair spring or main spring to make it perfect. They have a fatal lack of decision and they are always disappointing the high hopes which they are constantly raising in all who know them. They almost succeed, but not quite. Their vacillating purpose ever disappoints the sanguine expectations of their friends and ruins all their plans.

Truth, ability, sincerity, faithfulness to duty, spotless character—all these are indispensable to the young man or young woman who would carve out a career; but if enthusiasm, the joy and glory of labour, the divine spark that lifts it out of the commonplace, that makes man in a special sense at one with the Divine Will, if this power be lacking, life will lack its greatest charm.

The martyrs, the inventors, the artists, the musicians, the poets, the great writers, the heroes, the pioneers of civilisation, the movers of every great enterprise—those of every race and clime, in every age of the world, who have led man upward from the dawn of history to the twentieth century, have been enthusiasts.

If you cannot throw yourself with your whole soul into your work, whatever it may be, it will lack that vitalising quality which alone can lift it beyond mediocrity. It will not bear the stamp of individuality; it will be perfunctory, commonplace. There will be nothing to distinguish it from the production of thousands of other half-hearted workers.

Enthusiasm is the soul of work, and of life itself; the young man or young woman who feels no thrill of joy in daily labour, who is driven to it by the spur of necessity, who goes through it conscientiously, it may be, but merely as the performance of a disagreeable duty, is almost sure to fail in life. When young people work in such a spirit, there is something fatally wrong. Either they have mistaken their calling, and are wearing their lives away in a fruitless attempt to do that well which they should never have undertaken, or they need inward illumination. They want to be roused to the fact that the world needs their best work; that no half-hearted, indifferent efforts will justify them before their Creator, who has given us talents not to be folded in a napkin and returned to Him intact in the final rendering of accounts, but to be used, to be put out at interest, to be increased tenfold, twentyfold, a hundredfold, according to the ability of everyone.

No barrier, however formidable, no obstacle however insurmountable it may seem to the timid or faint-hearted, can bar the way to any youth possessed with enthusiasm for a high ideal.

Never before has the youth fired by enthusiasm had such an opportunity as he has to-day. It is the age of young men and young women. The world looks to them to be interpreters of new forms of truth and beauty. Secrets, jealously guarded by nature, are waiting to reveal themselves to the enthusiast who is ready to give his life to the work. Inventions foreshadowed to-day are waiting for the " passionate patience " of enthusiasm to develop them. Every occupation, every profession, every field of human endeavour, is clamorous for enthusiastic workers. Where shall we look for supply to meet the demand, if not in the ranks of youth, whose most irresistible charm is its bubbling enthusiasm? Thrice happy youth! It sees no darkness ahead—no defile that has no outlet—it forgets that there is such a thing as failure in the world, and believes that mankind has been waiting all these centuries for the youth of a new age.

" The world's interests," says Dr. Trumbull, " are, under God, in the hands of the young." " The most beautiful works of all art were done in youth," says Ruskin. " Almost everything," wrote Disraeli, " that is great has been done by youth." It was the youth Hercules, who performed the Twelve Labours. Alexander was a mere youth when he rolled back the Asiatic hordes that threatened to overwhelm European civilisation almost at its birth. Romulus founded Rome at twenty. Pitt and Bolingbroke were ministers almost before they were men. Gladstone was in Parliament in early manhood. Newton made some of his greatest discoveries before he was twenty-five. Keats died at twenty-five, Shelley at twenty-nine. Luther was a triumphant reformer at twenty-five. Ignatius Loyola founded his society at thirty. Whitefield and Wesley began their great revival when students at Oxford; and the former had made his influence felt throughout England before he was twenty-four. Victor Hugo wrote a tragedy at fifteen, and had taken three prizes at the Academy and gained the title of Master before he was twenty.

Enthusiasm is the compelling power that overcomes all obstacles. It is the being awake—tingling in every fibre of one's being—to do the work that his heart desires. It brooks no interference with the accomplishment of its object. Of what use was it to forbid the boy Händel to touch a musical instrument, or to forbid his going to school, lest he learn the gamut? He stole midnight interviews with a spinet in a secret attic. The boy Mozart toiled all day at disagreeable tasks, but stole at night to the church organ and poured out his very soul in music. The boy Bach copied whole books of studies by moonlight, for want of a candle churlishly denied. Nor was he disheartened when these copies were taken from him. Whipping and scolding only made Ole Bull's passionate childhood devotion to his violin more absorbing.

Indifference never leads armies that conquer, never models statues that live, nor breathes sublime music, nor harnesses the forces of nature, nor rears impressive architecture, nor moves the soul with poetry, nor the world with heroic philanthropies. Enthusiasm, as Charles Bell says of the hand, wrought the statue of Memnon and hung the brazen gates of Thebes. It fixed the mariner's trembling needle upon its axis, and first heaved the tremendous bar of the printing press. It opened the tubes for Galileo, until world after world swept before his vision; and it reefed the high topsail that rustled over Columbus in the morning breezes of the Bahamas. It has held the sword with which freedom has fought her battles; and poised the axe of the dauntless woodman as he opened the paths of civilisation; and turned the mystic leaves upon which Milton and Shakespeare inscribed their burning thoughts.

"Great designs," says Boyle, "are not accomplished without enthusiasm of some sort. It is the inspiration of everything great. Without it no man is to be feared, and with it no man is to be despised." It is the most potent factor in the accomplishment of all that is of value. It enters into every invention, every masterpiece of painting or sculpture, every great poem, essay or novel that holds the world breathless with admiration. It is a spiritual power. It has its birth among the higher potencies. You never find true enthusiasm in people who are always grovelling at the feet of the senses. In its very nature it is uplifting.

" The sense of this word among the Greeks," says Madame de Staël, " affords the noblest definition of it; enthusiasm signifies ' God in us.' " It is this God-spirit, animating men and women, that makes them forgetful of self, regardless of personal suffering, proof against ridicule and opposition, in the pursuit of their ideals.

Bunyan might have had his liberty; but not the separation from his poor blind daughter, not the needs of a family dependent upon him; not the love of liberty, nor the spur of ambition, could induce him to forego his plain preaching in public places. It was the enthusiasm of conviction which enabled this poor, ignorant, despised Bedford tinker to write his immortal allegory with such fascination that a whole world has read it.

Wendell Phillips has well said, " Enthusiasm is the life of the soul."

Horace Greeley said that the best product of labour is the high-minded workman with an enthusiasm for his work.

The clerks in a large mercantile house ridiculed a young companion, who began as an office boy, for doing so many things which did not belong to him to do. They laughed at his enthusiasm and interest in the business, saying that there was no sense in it, and that he would never get a cent for it. Not long afterwards, he was selected from all the employees and taken into the firm as a partner, and became in time manager of one of the largest concerns in the country.

Success is often due less to ability than to enthusiasm. The world makes way for the man who believes in his mission, who is dead in earnest. No matter what objections may be raised, no matter how dark the outlook, he believes in his power to transform into a reality, the vision which he alone sees.

It was enthusiasm which enabled Cyrus W. Field, after thirteen years of defeat, to lay the Atlantic cable. It was enthusiasm, in spite of carping critics, that sped Stephenson's locomotive to its triumphant goal. It was enthusiasm that sent Fulton's *Folly* on its successful way up the Hudson, to the dismay and consternation of his croaking detractors. It was enthusiasm that led Patrick Henry to utter those burning words of patriotic eloquence, which every schoolboy delights to declaim. It was enthusiasm or patriotic zeal that sent Sherman upon his victorious march to the sea.

It has been well said that all the liberties, reforms and political achievements of society have been gained by nations thrilling and throbbing to one great enthusiasm.

Enthusiasm will steady the heart and strengthen the will; it will give force to the thought, and nerve the hand until what was only a possibility becomes a reality. Do not be afraid of it. Let people call you an enthusiast, with an inflection of pity or half-contempt in the voice, if they wish. If a thing seems to be worth working for at all, if it appears to you of moment enough to challenge any effort, then put into what you do all the enthusiasm of which you are capable, regardless of criticism. He laughs best who laughs last. It is never the half-hearted, the coldly critical, the doubting and fearing, that accomplish the most.

He who respects his work so highly (and does it so reverently) that he cares little what the world thinks of it, is the man about whom the world comes at last to think a great deal.

Have an abiding faith in the value and importance of your work; of its indispensableness to the world. Have a solid faith in it as your peculiar mission, a rooted belief that it is the one thing to which you have been called.

With enthusiasm we may retain the youth of the spirit long after time has silvered the hair and robbed us of youthful vigour. It is the glory of old age as it is the charm of youth. It makes the old man even a more positive force than the young one. Gladstone at eighty had ten times the weight and power that any man of twenty-five would have with the same ideals. What a power was Bismarck at eighty. Lord Palmerston became prime minister of England a second time at seventy-five, and died prime minister at eighty-one. Galileo, at seventy-seven, blind and feeble, was working every day adapting the principle of the pendulum to clocks. The crown of age is its enthusiasm, and the respect paid to white hairs is reverence to a heart fervent in spite of the torpid influence of an enfeebled body. The "Odyssey" was the creation of a blind old man, but that old man was Homer. "I argue not against Heaven's hand or will," said Milton, when old, blind, and poor, "nor bate a jot of heart or hope; but still bear up and steer right onward." He was chilled with the frosts of time when he depicted the love of the first pair in Eden.

One of Dr. Johnson's best works, "The Lives of the Poets," was written when he was seventy-eight. Newton wrote new briefs to his "Principia" at eighty-three. Plato died writing, at eighty-one. Tom Scott began the study of Hebrew at eighty-six. Galileo was nearly seventy when he wrote on the laws of motion. James Watt learned German at eighty-five. Mrs. Somerville finished her "Molecular and Microscopic Science" at eighty-nine. Humboldt completed his "Cosmos" at ninety, a month before his death.

Like beauty, that bubbling enthusiasm which makes perpetual youth and sunshine in the heart is a divine gift, and yet it can be cultivated. To the admonition of the wise man, then—" With all thy getting, get understanding "—I would add this other, " With all thy getting, get enthusiasm." For it is this which gives new courage to the timid, new hope to the disheartened, and to those who are already strong and courageous it gives increase of power.

CHAPTER XV

"I MUST—THEREFORE I CAN"

"Doubt, fear, discouragement, are for the selfish, the passive, but not for me. God bids me go forth and do; and within I hear a voice which says I must—therefore I can."

"The nature which is all wood and straw is of no use; if we are to do well, we must have some iron in us."

"I know no such unquestionable badge and ensign of a sovereign mind as that tenacity of purpose which, through all changes of companions, or parties, or fortunes, changes never, bates no jot of heart or hope, but wearies out opposition and arrives at its port."

"I find nothing so singular in life as this, that everything opposing appears to lose its substance the moment one actually grapples with it."

AFTER his world-renowned passage of the Alps, Napoleon pressed forward with his army along the banks of the Aosta. The valley was rich in verdure, bright in the bloom of an Italian spring. The road wound past cottages, vineyards, and orchards, while to the right and the left rose the fir-clad Alps, their summits white with snow. All was elation as the soldiers swept enthusiastically onward, when suddenly word was passed from rank to rank that the valley, just ahead, converged to a precipitous, craggy gorge, almost filled by the river,

with barely room for a narrow road, and with
an impregnable Austrian fort, built on an almost
inaccessible rock and very strongly garrisoned,
commanding the pass and rendering farther advance apparently impossible. Even those war-
worn veterans looked at one another in consternation, and a hush as of death instantly succeeded the cheerful hum of enthusiastic voices.

But calmly, coolly, and without a moment's
hesitation, the young leader prepared to cope with
what seemed an insuperable difficulty. Creeping
by a narrow goat path to an elevated point opposite the fort, he lay behind some stunted bushes,
and through his telescope studied, with minutest
care, the frowning batteries and the rocks around.
He noted one crag, towering above the fort, to
which a cannon might be drawn, making the bas-
tions untenable. Far up the opposite cliff, out
of range of cannon, he saw a narrow shelf by
which a man might possibly pass.

Returning, he at once ordered an advance by
this path, in single file, leading the horses. The
Austrians, in chagrin, saw thirty-five thousand
men, in airy line, crawl safely past them, like a
huge serpent, seeming to cling to the very face of
the rock.

"Upon the summit, quite exhausted with days
and nights of sleeplessness," says Abbott, "Napoleon laid himself down in the shadow of the

rock and fell asleep. The long line filed carefully and silently by, each soldier hushing his comrade, that the repose of their beloved chieftain might not be disturbed. Every foot trod softly, and each eye, in passing, was riveted upon the slender form and pale and wasted cheek of the sleeping Napoleon."

The Austrian commander wrote to General Melas that he had seen thirty-five thousand men and four thousand horses creep along the face of Mount Albaredo, but that not one single cannon had passed or could pass beneath the guns of his fort. But, even while he was writing, half of the French artillery, by another plan of Napoleon, was advancing down the valley. In the deep darkness of midnight in that narrow gorge, the invaders spread hay and straw along the road, bound coats and straw on the tires of their gun-carriages, and drew the well-oiled wheels in muffled silence by, within half pistol-shot of the guns. On the second night, the last cannon was drawn past by the brawny arms of the Frenchmen, and soon the fort was forced to capitulate.

Any other leader might have done the same thing, but no one else has done it, before or since. It was merely one of the many " miracles " of tireless, unshrinking endeavour whose sum made up the overwhelming victory of Marengo, June 14, 1800.

"It is curious," says John Foster, "when a firm and decisive spirit is recognised, to see how the space clears around a man and leaves room and freedom." An indomitable will, an inflexible purpose, finds a way or makes one.

Yet we must not expect to overcome a stubborn fact by a stubborn will. Will power is necessary to success, and, other things being equal, the greater the will power, the grander and more complete the success; *but determination must be tempered with discretion, and supported with knowledge and common sense, or it will only lead us to run our heads against posts.* We merely have the right to assume that we can do anything within the limit of our utmost faculty, strength, and endurance. Obstacles permanently insurmountable bar our progress in some directions, but, in any direction in which we may reasonably hope and attempt to go, we shall find that the obstacles are not insurmountable. A will strong enough to keep one continually striving for things not wholly beyond his powers will carry him in time very far toward his chosen goal. The strong-willed, intelligent, persistent man will find or make a way where, in the nature of things, a way can be found or made.

"What has been done can be done again," said the boy with no chance, who became Lord Beaconsfield, England's great prime minister. "I am not a slave, I am not a captive, and by energy I can overcome greater obstacles." He had Hebrew blood in his veins; was well versed in the annals of his race; and was endowed with the spirit to look back across the centuries of Jewish persecution to the ages when his people were the beloved of Jehovah, when Joseph and Daniel rose to honour in the country of the stranger. Gay, handsome, audacious, the youth was asked by Lord Melbourne, the great prime minister, what he wished to be. "Prime minister of England," he replied. Rebuffed, scorned, ridiculed, hissed down in the House of Commons, he asserted calmly that the time should come when they would hear him. Three defeats in parliamentary elections daunted him not in the least. He pushed his way up through the lower classes, up through the middle classes, up through the upper classes, until he stood self-poised upon the topmost round of political and social power, forcing his leadership upon that very party whose prejudices were deepest against his race, and which had an utter contempt for self-made men and interlopers.

Disraeli is but one of a myriad heroic spirits who might have said with a character in one of Ben Jonson's plays: "When I once take the humour of a thing, I am like your tailor's needle, I go through with it."

Balzac's father tried to discourage his son from

the pursuit of literature. "Do you know," said he, "that in literature a man must be either a king or a beggar?" "Very well," replied the boy, "I will be a king." His parents left him to his fate in a garret. For ten years he fought terrible battles with hardship and poverty, but won a great victory at last.

Benjamin Franklin had this tenacity of purpose in a wonderful degree. When he started in the printing business in Philadelphia, he carried his material through the streets on a wheelbarrow. He hired one room for his office, workroom, and sleeping room. He found a formidable rival in the city and invited him to his room. Pointing to a piece of bread from which he had just eaten his dinner, he said: "Unless you can live cheaper than I can you cannot starve me out."

The astronomer Kepler, whose name can never die, was kept in constant anxieties, and told fortunes by astrology for a livelihood, saying that that science, as the daughter of astronomy, ought to keep her mother. He had to accept all sorts of service; he made almanacs and worked for anyone who would pay him. But he had the kind of will that makes a way. Humphry Davy had but a slender chance to acquire great scientific knowledge, yet he had true mettle in him, and he made even old pans, kettles, and bottles contribute to his success, as he experimented and studied in the attic of the apothecary store where he worked.

A sun-browned country youth called on Bishop Simpson, then president of Asbury University. His plain clothes led the bishop to ask him what he had to depend upon. "My two hands, sir," replied the boy, who afterward became a United States senator.

When Louisa M. Alcott was first dreaming of her power, her father handed her a manuscript, one day, that had been rejected by James T. Fields, editor of the "Atlantic Monthly," with the message:

"Tell Louisa to stick to her teaching; she can never succeed as a writer."

"Tell him I *will* succeed as a writer, and some day I shall write for the 'Atlantic.'" The day came when work of hers was accepted by that magazine. She earned two hundred thousand dollars by her pen. "Twenty years ago," she wrote in her diary, "I resolved to make the family independent if I could. At forty, that is done. My debts are all paid, even the outlawed ones, and we have enough to be comfortable. It has cost me my health, perhaps."

When told by his physicians that he must die, Douglas Jerrold replied: "What! Leave a family of helpless children? I won't die." He kept his word, and lived for years.

" We go forth," said Emerson, " austere, dedicated, believing in the iron links of Destiny, and will not turn on our heels to save our lives. A book, a bust, or only the sound of a name shoots a spark through the nerves, and we suddenly believe in will. We cannot hear of personal vigour of any kind, great power of performance, without fresh resolution."

The youth who starts out in life determined to make the most of his eyes and let nothing escape him which he can possibly use for his own advancement; who keeps his ears open for every sound that can help him on his way; who keeps his hands open that he may clutch every opportunity; who is ever on the alert for everything which can help him to get on in the world; who seizes every experience in life and grinds it up into paint for his great life's picture; who keeps his heart open that he may catch every noble impulse and everything which may inspire him; who possesses a will determined to beat and hammer its way through all obstacles, never to tire, never to acknowledge failure, but to drive on and ever on, conquering environment, rising superior to circumstances, will reach his desires and win his goal. He will be sure to make his life successful; there are no " ifs " or " ands " about it.

Constant struggle to win success from inhospitable surroundings, is the price of all great achievements. The boy or girl who would attain a successful manhood or womanhood must prepare for the work of life, from the outset, by battling bravely against the obstacles that would bar progress. Young men and young women starting out in life should look in the face the fact that obstacles are not only inevitable, but that they are an indispensable part of the training for honourable success. Their conquest measures the price of all achievement.

Patience, perseverance, undaunted courage, loyalty to high ideals and the dominant purpose of life, are the tests of royal manhood and womanhood, the steps that lead to the accomplishment of the world's best work.

Every condition, says W. E. Channing, be it what it may, has hardships, hazards, pains; we try to escape them; we pine for a sheltered lot, for a smooth path, for cheering friends, and unbroken success. But Providence ordains storms, disasters, hostilities, sufferings; and the great question whether we shall live to any purpose or not, whether we shall grow strong in mind and heart, or be weak and pitiable, depends on nothing more than our use of the adverse circumstances. Outward evils are designed to school our passions, and to rouse our faculties and virtues into intenser action. Sometimes they seem to create new powers. Difficulty is the element, and resistance the true work of men. Self-culture never goes on faster than when embarrassed circumstances, the opposition of men or the elements, unexpected changes of the times, or other forms of suffering, instead of disheartening, throw us on our inward resources, turn us for strength to God, clear up to us the great purpose of life, and inspire calm resolution. No greatness or goodness is worth much, unless tried in these fires.

Grit is the grindstone saying to the axe: "You are hard, are you? Well, I am harder and more stubborn; and I will wear you out with the grit that is in my substance and fibre." Garrison had grit when he said, in the "Liberator," "I am in earnest, I will not equivocate, I will not excuse, I will not retreat a single inch, and I will be heard." The grit of that grindstone wore out a thousand axes.

"At last I am here!" exclaimed a determined-looking man who had just entered, addressing General Dumas, seated in the house of a French physician, on the German side of the River Niemen, December 13, 1812. Dumas scanned the stranger with a suspicious glance. He was wrapped in a large cloak. His hair and beard were long, unkempt, and singed with fire; his features were wan and thin and black with powder; but his eyes gleamed with dauntless purpose, and his entire bearing showed that he was a man of iron.

" What, General Dumas! " he exclaimed. " Do you not know me? "

" No," replied the general; " who are you? "

" I am the rear guard of the Grand Army, Marshal Ney," replied the visitor.

General Dumas looked again, long and earnestly, and at length said, half to himself, " It is indeed, Ney! "

On the morning of that very day, the wretched remnants of Napoleon's grand army, some thirty thousand in all, escaped from Russian territory and crossed the Niemen. The " Old Guard " numbered but three hundred men, but they still marched proudly as of old. Ney, who had survived four rear guards of some five thousand men each, managed to collect seven hundred fresh men and held the pursuing thousands in check all day long while the army filed across the bridge. His little band dwindled until he had but thirty soldiers in line. With these falling one by one he fought until the bridge was clear. The men rushed across, but Ney walked coolly backward, fired the last bullet at the Russians, threw his gun into the river, and left the enemy's territory last of all. What wonder that such a man was called " the bravest of the brave! "

At Toulon, in 1793, Napoleon called for some

one who could write to prepare an order at his dictation. A private stepped forward, rested his paper upon the breastwork, and began to write. Just as he finished the first page an English cannon ball struck the ground near them and scattered dirt over them and the paper. "Thank you!" exclaimed the private, " we shall need no more sand upon this page."

" Young man," said Napoleon, " what can I do for you? "

" Everything," said the soldier, as he touched his left shoulder; " you can change this worsted into an epaulet."

A few days later, Napoleon sent the man to reconnoitre the trenches of the enemy, and asked him to adopt some disguise, as the peril was great.

" Never!" exclaimed the soldier. " Do you take me for a spy? I will go in my uniform, though I should never return."

He returned unharmed, and his commander at once recommended him for promotion. He became Marshal Junot.

The London " Times " was an insignificant sheet published by John Walter, and was steadily losing money. John Walter, Jr., then only twenty-seven years old, begged his father to give him full control of the paper. With many misgivings, the father finally consented. The young journalist began to remodel the establishment and to introduce new ideas everywhere. The paper had not attempted to mould public opinion, and had no individuality or character of its own. The audacious young editor boldly attacked every wrong, even the government, when he thought it corrupt. Thereupon the public customs, printing, and the government advertisements were withdrawn. The father was in utter dismay. The son, he was sure, would ruin the paper and himself. But no remonstrance could swerve him from his purpose to give the world a great journal which should have weight, character, individuality, and independence. The public soon saw that a new power stood behind the " Times "; that its articles meant business; that new life and new blood and new ideas had been infused into the insignificant sheet; that a man with brains and push and tenacity of purpose stood at the helm—a man who could make a way when he could not find one. Among other new features foreign dispatches were introduced, and they appeared in the " Times " several days before their appearance in the government organs. The " leading article " also was introduced to stay. But the aggressive editor antagonised the government, and his foreign dispatches were all stopped at the outpost, while those of the ministerial journalists were allowed to proceed. But nothing could daunt this resolute young spirit. At enormous expense he employed special couriers. Every obstacle put in his way, and all opposition from the government, only added to his determination to succeed. Enterprise, push, and grit were behind the " Times," and nothing could stay its progress.

Emerson says: " Shallow men believe in luck, believe in circumstances; it was somebody's name, or he happened to be there at the time, or it was so then, and another day it would have been otherwise. Strong men believe in cause and effect. All successful men have agreed in one thing—they have been causationists. They believe that things go not by luck but by law; that there is not a weak or a cracked link in the chain that joins the first and the last of things."

When the prizes of life shall be awarded by the Supreme Judge, who knows our weaknesses and frailties, the distance we have run, the weights we have carried, the handicaps will be all taken into account. Not the distance we have run, but the obstacles we have overcome, the disadvantages under which we have made the race, will decide the prizes. The poor wretch who has plodded along against unknown temptations, the poor woman who has buried her sorrows in her silent heart and sewed her weary way through life, those who have suffered abuse in silence, and who have been unrecognised or despised by their fellow-runners, will often receive the greater prize.

CHAPTER XVI

COURAGE AT THE STICKING-POINT

> We fail!
> But screw your courage to the sticking-place,
> And we'll not fail.
>
> SHAKESPEARE.

Perseverance and tact are the two great qualities most valuable for all men who would mount, but especially for those who have to step out of the crowd.—DISRAELI.

PERSEVERANCE," says Carlyle, " is the very hinge of all virtues. On looking over the world, the cause of nine parts in ten of the lamentable failures which occur in men's undertakings, and darken and degrade so much of their history, lies not in the want of talents, or the will to use them, but in the vacillating and desultory mode of using them, in flying from object to object, in starting away at each little disgust, and thus applying the force which might conquer any one difficulty to a series of difficulties so large that no human force can conquer them. The smallest brook on earth, by continuing to run, has hollowed out for itself a considerable valley. The wildest tempest overturns a few cottages, uproots a few trees, and leaves, after a short space, no mark behind it.

Commend me, therefore, to the Dutch virtue of perseverance. Without it, all the rest are little better than fairy gold, which glitters in your purse, but, when taken to the market, proves to be slate or cinders."

He who can be beaten, but not broken; be victorious, but not vainglorious; strive and contend for the prize, and win it honestly or lose it cheerfully; use every power in the race, and yet never wrest an undue advantage or win an unlawful mastery—he it is who " by a life heroic conquers fate."

When Napoleon reached Krasnoe, in the terrible retreat from Moscow, he had left but nine thousand men, half-famished, exhausted, and almost without arms, and was hard pressed by eighty thousand well-fed, well-armed Russians, under Kutusoff. The least delay would enable other Russian soldiers to gain possession of rivers and defiles ahead, and possibly to cut off his retreat. But Ney and Davoust, who were following miles behind to check the Russian march, had not been heard from for several days. To turn back seemed certain destruction, but Napoleon was not the man to desert his comrades in their time of peril. The order was given to return.

" Set out immediately," said he to General Rapp, pointing to a powerful body of Russians which occupied a strong position on his right;

" and, during the darkness, attack that body with the bayonet. This is the first time the enemy has exhibited such audacity. I am about to make him repent it in such a way that he will never again approach my headquarters."

But, after a moment's reflection, he recalled Rapp, saying: " No, let Roguet and his division go. Remain where you are. I must not have you killed. I shall have occasion for you at Dantzic."

Desperate was the battle, all through the night and until two o'clock the next day, when Davoust appeared, but no tidings of Ney could be gained. The westward march through snow and icy winds was resumed, but at the Dnieper Ney was heard from, and a force of five thousand men returned and rescued him.

" When I was carrying the order to Roguet, to turn back and aid Davoust and Ney," said Rapp, " I could not help feeling astonished that Napoleon, surrounded by eighty thousand of the enemy, whom he was going to attack the next day with nine thousand, should have so little doubt about his safety as to be thinking of what he should have to do at Dantzic, a city from which he was separated by the winter, two hostile armies, famine, and one hundred and eighty leagues of distance."

But it was this very absence of doubt, this cool, deliberate, far-reaching forethought, which, supported by lion courage and bulldog tenacity, alone enabled Napoleon to save even a remnant of the Grand Army. He did, indeed, find use for Rapp after they had crossed the Russian frontier.

"Who first consults wisely, then resolves firmly, and then executes his purpose with inflexible perseverance, undismayed by those petty difficulties which daunt a weaker spirit—that man can advance to eminence in any line."

If a youth has not the quality of persistence in his nature; if he hesitates before obstacles; if he cannot make difficulties bend to his purpose, or cause opposition to give way, he will, at best, make but a partial success in life. He may have shining qualities of nature; may be intellectual, intelligent, industrious, courteous; but, if he is wanting in persistence, that dogged determination which follows its purpose to death or victory, he lacks the one sure foundation for his life structure.

There is, perhaps, no other thing which will advance youth so rapidly as to gain the reputation of being persistent—of never giving up. Such a reputation is a letter of credit which is honoured of all mankind, and is of far more value than an inherited fortune in the hands of a weak-minded person.

There is a never-failing demand for the man who sees longevity in his cause, no matter what others see, or what others say, and has the pluck and tenacity of purpose, amid ridicule and defeat, to await the issue. It is the home stretch that tests the man. It is he who possesses the ability to abide by his determination, whose staying power will not allow him to loosen his grip on his work, who insures permanent benefit.

"Does he keep at it? Is he doggedly persistent? Does he hold on when others let go? Does he stick to it through thick and thin, when others give up? Is he the most courageous when others are afraid? Does he stiffen when others begin to weaken?" The young man of whom these questions can be answered in the affirmative will make a way where he does not find one. He will succeed in spite of his failures.

A poor lad in London determined to visit every office and place of business in the city until he should find a situation, no matter how long it might take. After persisting in this for a time which would have utterly discouraged most boys, he called at an office where he was told that they never took boys who had not had a situation before, and was asked who sent him there. The old gentleman who was chief in authority was so pleased at the lad's pluck when he told that he was calling at every office and should continue to do so until he found a situation, that he told the boy to go home and write him a letter in his best hand and he would see what he could do for him. Many a boy has lost a situation by bad handwriting, bad

spelling, or an unbusiness-like letter; but this persevering youth's letter was neat, and otherwise
satisfactory, and he got the situation.   He proved
a valuable boy, and has been with the firm ever
since.

The following story has no written sequel, but
it stands very well without it :

" ' Do you want a boy ? ' asked an applicant of
the magnate of the office, standing before him cap
in hand.

" ' Nobody wants a boy,' replied the magnate.

" ' Do you need a boy ? ' asked the applicant,
nowise abashed.

" ' Nobody needs a boy.'

" The boy would not give up.

" ' Well, say, mister,' he inquired, ' do you have
to have a boy ? '

" ' I'm sorry to say we do,' said the man, ' and
I guess you're about what we want.' "

The race is not always to the swift.   The persistent tortoise will outrun the timid hare.   It
is said that the ant will repair his dwelling as often
as the mischievous foot crushes it; the spider will
exhaust life itself, before he will live without a
web; the bee can be decoyed from his labour neither
by plenty nor scarcity.   If summer be abundant,
it toils none the less; if it be parsimonious of
flowers, the tiny labourer sweeps a wider circle,
and still gathers honey busily.   Many a moral can

we learn from these peoples, exceeding little and exceeding wise.

Timor, the Tartar, being forced to flee from his enemies, hid in an old ruined building. As the weary hours wore away, he sought to keep his mind from his troubles by watching an ant carrying a grain of corn larger than itself up a high wall. Again and again the little creature tugged away at its heavy load; but, before it reached its destination, the grain fell again to the ground. Sixty-nine times the kernel of corn fell, when partly up the wall; but the seventieth time the ant reached the top with its precious burden. Timor never forgot the lesson of perseverance and courage which this little creature taught him.

The romance of perseverance is one of the most fascinating subjects in history. The stories of those who have had the genius of persistency, even though mediocre in ability, read like the " Arabian Nights." Tenacity of purpose has been characteristic of all great characters who have left their mark on the world.

Perseverance, it has been said, is the statesman's brain, the warrior's sword, the inventor's secret, the scholar's " Open Sesame."

" Persistency," says E. P. Whipple, " is the quality separating first-rate genius from all the other rates." Persistency is to talent what steam is to the engine. It is the driving force by which the machine accomplishes the work for which it was intended. A great deal of persistency, with a very little talent, can be counted on to go farther than a great deal of talent without persistency.

"Many a genius has been slow of growth. Oaks that flourish for a thousand years do not spring up into beauty like a reed." The growth of the American aloe is, for many years, almost imperceptible. Then, all at once, when the time comes, there is a crisis. The plant shoots up a tall stalk hung with innumerable flowers. Even so is it often with those whom the world has come at last to honour.

"Generally speaking," said Sydney Smith, " the life of all truly great men has been a life of intense and incessant labour. They have commonly passed the first half of life in the gross darkness of indigent humility—overlooked, mistaken, condemned by weaker men—thinking while others slept, reading while others rioted, feeling something within that told them they should not always be kept down among the dregs of the world. And then, when their time has come, and some little accident has given them their first occasion, they have burst out into the light and glory of public life, rich with the spoils of time, and mighty in all the labours and struggles of the mind."

Von Moltke, the greatest master of strategy, perhaps, that the world has seen, stuck to his task until he was sixty-six years of age, before his great opportunity came.

Persistency has been characteristic of our military and naval heroes. Grant, even when only sixteen, had a conviction that to retreat was fatal; when he undertook anything, he was determined to follow it to the very end; so, when he said, "I can do that," he did it. A story related by President Lincoln to an army officer, one evening at the theatre ten days before his assassination, shows the value placed by the President upon this trait in his "unconditional surrender" general. "I want to tell you a story about Grant and the mule," said he. "When Grant was a youngster, the circus came to his town, and he went to the tanner and asked him for a ticket. The hard-headed tanner refused him, so Grant, doing the next best thing (as I did myself), crawled under the tent. The ring master had an ugly mule, which no one could ride, and offered a prize of a dollar to any boy who would ride the animal around the ring, without being thrown off. Quite a number of boys tried it without success. Finally young Grant ventured out from behind the seats where he was viewing the show, and said to the ring master, 'I'd like to try that mule.' 'All right,' said the ring master, and Grant got on, and rode nearly round the ring, but was finally thrown over the animal's head. The boy got up, threw off his coat, and said, ' Let me try that again.' This time he got on with his back to the head of the animal, and clung with all his might to the tail, and, in spite of all the animal could do, held on, and won the dollar. Now," added Lincoln, " Grant will do the same at Richmond. He will hang on, he will never give up. He will try again and again till he succeeds."

Stone-wall men, like Grant and Jackson in the Civil War, and like Napoleon before them, have never known when they were beaten. Neither bayonets, nor bullets, nor shells, nor torpedoes, nor mines, nor defeat itself have been able to stay their progress. They were masters of perseverance—the stern stuff

"That wins each godlike act, and plucks success
    Even from the spear-proof crest of rugged danger."

Napoleon used to say that the kind of valour he prized was " two-o'clock-in-the-morning courage." No doubt this kind of valour was of great service to the emperor ; yet one questions whether, after all, he could have attained to the eminence to which he rose without an extraordinary share of what a modern writer has called " five-o'clock-in-the-afternoon courage." " After the nerves have been worn and the patience exhausted by the labour and irritations of a long day, it needs a high type of energy and persistence for a man to maintain his purpose, to keep his spirit up to the mark, and not to relax his efforts in the very last hour of the day's work. The writer has more than once seen a choice business opportunity slip from the grasp of a man who should have held it, simply because he lacked five-o'clock-in-the-afternoon courage; and if the secrets of the committee rooms of Congress should be published, it would be found that many a great measure has failed simply because the man who had charge of it weakened at the last moment. If he had hung on a little longer, he would have carried his point. The French say that it is the first step that costs, but it is the last step that counts. The Apostle Paul understood this when he told the Ephesian Christians, ' having done all, to stand.' "

Where will you find five-o'clock-in-the-afternoon courage better exhibited than in the heroic perseverance of Livingston? Twenty-seven attacks of fever, innumerable assaults from savages, the lonely journeys in the jungle, brought the brave traveller many a time to the verge of the grave, and reduced him to a skeleton; but never in the least degree affected his dogged determination. When his men positively refused to accompany him farther, and threatened to leave him in the desert, he said: " After using all my powers of persuasion, I declared that, if they returned, I should go on alone; and, returning to my little tent, I lifted up my heart to Him who hears the sighing of the soul. Presently the head man came in. 'Do not be disheartened,' he said. 'Our remarks were only made on account of the injustice of these people. We will never leave you. Wherever you lead we will follow.'"

George Stephenson was not the inventor of the iron rail, nor of the idea of a steam-driven vehicle running upon a railroad and carrying its own water and fuel; why is it that it was he who was called the father of the modern locomotive, and not Trevethick, in whose earlier engine these leading features were present? Was it not that same five-o'clock-in-the-afternoon courage that made the difference between the two men. Trevethick became discouraged and gave up; Stephenson, by careful study, by noticing the defects of others, and seeking a remedy, by careful attention to details, when a less persevering man would have been sure to fail, finally, in 1815, produced an engine, "The Puffing Billy," that was really serviceable and economical. But his work was by no means done. He had a hard battle to fight still, before he could conquer. He was the only man in the world who had faith in the ultimate use of this method of travel. However, he persevered, and, in spite of all obstacles, in 1830 he had a locomotive, "The Rocket," in essential principles the same as to-day, running on the Liverpool and Manchester Railway, and the success of his ideas was established.

"The only merit to which I lay claim," said Hugh Miller, "is that of patient research—a merit in which whoever will may rival or surpass me; and this humble faculty of patience, when rightly developed, may lead to more extraordinary development of ideas than even genius itself."

"When we go about our work earnestly and perseveringly," wrote Goethe, "it often happens that, although we have to tack about again and again, we get ahead of those who are helped by wind and tide." He who is helped by the wind and tide of genius will never accomplish anything if he lacks persistence. Stick-to-itiveness and dogged pertinacity are fundamental qualities in every profession, in every trade and calling. They are to all the other qualifications what the string is to the necklace, that which unites individual jewels into an effective and beautiful whole.

Goldsmith thought a few lines a good day's work. He was seven years evolving "The Deserted Village." "By a long habit of writing," he declared, "one acquires a greatness of thinking and a mastery of manner which holiday writers, with ten times the genius, may vainly attempt to equal."

" How hard I worked at that tremendous short-hand, and all improvement appertaining to it!" said Dickens. " I will only add to what I have already written of my perseverance at this time of my life, and of a patient and continuous energy which then began to be matured within me, and which I know to be the strong point of my character, if it have any strength at all, that there, on looking back, I find the source of my success."

The best romance that ever came from an American pen—" The Scarlet Letter "—was produced under trials and hardships which would have discouraged a less noble soul than Hawthorne's. Drudgery, drudgery, drudgery, was the record of all his efforts. Nothing was too trivial for entry in his notebook in the preparation of this wonderful work. For twenty years he worked on and on, alone and unrecognised. But he kept saying to himself, " My turn will come; " and he persisted until it did come.

How Bulwer wrestled with the fates to change his apparent destiny! His first novel was a failure; his early poems were failures; and his youthful speeches provoked the ridicule of his opponents. But he fought his way to eminence through ridicule and defeat.

The characters in Sheridan's " School for

Scandal," which seem to have been the result of a stroke of genius, thrown off at white heat, were altered and recast again and again. Many of the speeches put into the mouths of Sir Peter and Lady Teazle were shifted and remodelled from what they were in the first draft, till hardly two words stand in the same order in which they were originally written. Oliver Wendell Holmes never tired of mending or improving his verses. Longfellow elaborated his poems very slowly, and weighed every word with the utmost care before writing it down. He sent beautiful manuscripts to the printer, with hardly an erasure, but they often contained only a very little of the original draft. It is said that the whole of the " Divine Tragedy " was rewritten after most of it was in type. Emerson revised his writing with the greatest care. He was diligent, slow, and painstaking. Even his most striking sentences, which seem to be the scintillations of genius, were written and rewritten with persistent labour. His works were carefully revised again and again, portions omitted and new matter added. He was unsparing in his corrections. His manuscripts which have been preserved are crowded with erasures and corrections. There is scarcely a page that is not covered with these evidences of diligent revision. One of his biographers tells us that " his apples were sorted over and over again, until only the very rarest, the most perfect, were kept. It did not matter that those thrown away were very good, and helped to make clear the possibilities of the orchard; they were unmercifully cast aside. Consequently, his essays were very slowly elaborated, wrought out through days and months, and even years of patient labour."

Ariosto wrote his " Description of a Tempest " sixteen different ways. He spent ten years on his " Orlando Furioso," and sold only one hundred copies at 15 pence each. The proof of Burke's " Letters to a Noble Lord " (one of the sublimest things in all literature) went back to the publisher so changed and blotted with corrections that the printer absolutely refused to correct it, and it was entirely reset. Adam Tucker spent eighteen years on the " Light of Nature." A great naturalist spent eight years on the " Anatomy of the Day Fly." Thoreau's New England pastoral, " A Week on the Concord and Merrimac Rivers," was an entire failure. Seven hundred of the one thousand copies printed were returned from the publishers. Thoreau wrote in his diary: " I have some nine hundred volumes in my library, seven hundred of which I wrote myself." Yet, he says, he took up his pen with as much determination as before.

" Whoever is resolved to excel in painting, or, indeed in any other art," said Reynolds, " must

bring all his mind to bear upon that one object
from the moment that he rises till he goes to bed.
Upon being asked how long it took him to paint a
certain picture, Sir Joshua replied, "All my life."

"The pit rose at me!" exclaimed Edmund
Kean, in a wild tumult of emotion, as he rushed
home to his trembling wife. "Mary, you shall
ride in your carriage yet, and Charles shall go to
Eton!" He had been so terribly in earnest with
the study of his profession that he had at length
made a mark on his generation. He was a little,
dark man, with a voice naturally harsh, but he
determined, when young, to play the character of
Sir Giles Overreach, in Massinger's drama, as no
other man had ever played it. By a persistency
that nothing seemed able to daunt, he so trained
himself to play the character that his success,
when it did come, was overwhelming, and all London was at his feet.

Sothern, the great actor, said that the early
part of his theatrical career was spent in getting
dismissed for incompetency. Talma, one of the
greatest actors France has produced, was hissed
off the stage when he first appeared on it.

Lacordaire, one of the greatest preachers of
modern times, acquired his celebrity only after
repeated failures. It was said by Montalembert
on his first public appearance in the Church of St.
Roch—"He failed completely, and, on coming

out, everyone said, 'Though he be a man of talent, he will never be a preacher.'" Again and again he tried, until he succeeded; only two years after his *début,* Lacordaire was preaching in Notre Dame to audiences such as few French orators have addressed since the time of Bossuet and Massillon.

"It is all very well," said Charles James Fox, "to tell me that a young man has distinguished himself by a brilliant first speech. He may go on, or he may be satisfied with his first triumph; but show me a young man who has not succeeded at first, and nevertheless has gone on, and I will back that young man to do better than most of those who have succeeded at the first trial."

"It is in me, and it shall come out!" cried Sheridan, when, having failed at his first speech in parliament, he was told that he would never make an orator. He became known as one of the foremost orators of his day.

When President Pierce made his *début* at the bar, he broke down completely. Although deeply mortified, he was not discouraged. He said that he would try the experiment nine hundred and ninety-nine times more; and then, if he failed, he would repeat it for the thousandth time. He furnishes but one more illustration of the cases in which opposing circumstances have created strength.

" There's nothing like giving a boy a little encouragement, once in a while," said a wealthy New York merchant the other day, as related in *Puck*. " I know I owe a great deal to a remark a crabbed old farmer made to me when I was quite small. I was trying to split a cross-grained hickory log, and, as our wood-pile was close by the roadside, my efforts attracted the notice of the farmer, who stopped his team. I was greatly flattered by his attention, because he was the crossest and surliest man in town, and never took any notice of boys, except to sit in his orchard with a shotgun in his hand when the apples were ripe. So I put in my best strokes, and covered my hands with blisters, but the log refused to split. I hated to be beaten, but there seemed no help for it. The old man noticed my chagrin.

" ' Humph! I thought you'd hev to give it up!', he said, with a chuckle.

" Those words were all I needed. I made no reply; but the way the axe went into that log was a revelation. As I drove it into the *knots,* they yielded. There was a cheerful crackle, the gap widened, and soon the halves lay before me, and the farmer drove off discomfited. But I never forgot it. When I first went into business, I made mistakes, as every young man will. But, whenever I got caught in a doubtful enterprise, I remembered that my friends were standing around waiting for the chance to say: 'I thought you'd have to give it up!' In spite of himself, that old farmer gave me the keynote of my success. So you see that, if a boy has any grit in him, he is bound to profit by the right sort of encouragement—and a well placed sneer is sometimes worth more than a barrel of taffy."

Success is not to be measured by what a man accomplishes, but by the opposition he has encountered, and the courage with which he has maintained the struggle against overwhelming odds.

Reserves which carry us through great emergencies are the result of long working and long waiting. Collyer declares that reserves mean to a man also achievement—" the power to do the grandest thing possible to your nature when you feel you must, or some precious thing will be lost; to do well always, but best in the crisis on which all things turn; to stand the strain of a long fight, and still find you have something left, and so never to know you are beaten, because you never are beaten." Every defeat is a Waterloo to him who has no reserves. It is staying power which enables a man to clutch his purpose with an iron grip.

When you know you are on the right track, do not let any failures dim your vision or discourage you, for you cannot tell how close you may be to victory. The most perilous hour of a person's life is when he is tempted to despond. The man who loses his courage loses all; but it matters not how poor he may be, how much pushed by circumstances, how much deserted by friends, how much lost to the world, if he only keeps his courage, holds up his head, works on with his hands, and with an unconquerable will determines to be and to do what becomes a man, for all will then be well. It is nothing outside of men that kills, but what is within, that makes or unmakes.

Colton declares that, in moments of despondency, even Shakespeare thought himself no poet, and Raphael doubted his right to be called a painter. But Shakespeare wrote and Raphael painted. They were too great to give up in the face of the inevitable disappointments and vexations and fatigues incident to their careers. "Genius," says E. P. Whipple, "is ever victorious over drudgery, refusing to submit to the weariness and the deferred hope which attend upon vast designs."

Columbus, in the journal kept upon his most memorable voyage, day after day wrote these simple but sublime words: "This day we sailed westward, which was our course." Hope might rise and fall, terror and dismay seize upon the crew at the mysterious variations of the compass, but Columbus, unappalled, pushed on due west.

Sail westward, if that be your course, day and night; time and inexorable will, let those be your chart and compass upon the labouring seas whereon you sail. Sail westward, which is your course, through sunshine and storm, through hurricane and tempest, through sleet and rain, though with a leaky ship, and with a crew in mutiny. Some night you shall catch a gleam of light betokening your nearness to the land of your long search.

CHAPTER XVII

COURTESY, TIDINESS, AND HEART SUNSHINE

I

THE monk, Basle, according to a quaint old legend, died while under the ban of excommunication by the pope, and was sent in charge of an angel to find his proper place in the nether world. But his genial disposition and his great conversational powers won friends wherever he went. The fallen angels adopted his manner, and even the good angels went a long way to see him and live with him. He was removed to the lowest depths of Hades, but with the same result. His inborn politeness and kindness of heart were irresistible, and he seemed to change the hell into a heaven. At length the angel returned with the monk, saying that no place could be found in which to punish him. He still remained the same Basle. So his sentence was revoked, and he was sent to Heaven and canonized as a saint.

"Certain it is," said Mrs. Mary A. Livermore, "that the best passport to society a young man or woman can have, next to a clean character, is the possession of fine manners. Young people who are awkward, shy, and ill at ease in the society of others, neither give nor receive pleasure. Their evident embarrassment is painful to those who witness it as well as to themselves." This shyness and awkwardness are largely the result of a sensitive self-consciousness, which can and must be overcome if their lives are to be full, joyous, and free, as they were meant to be. What is self-consciousness but a kind of egotism, which makes its victim feel that he is the centre of observation, wherever he goes, that all eyes are upon him, taking note of his every act, that all ears are open to hear and all hearers ready to criticise what he says. *Do not think of yourself.* This is the simple negative formula for ridding yourself of self-consciousness. Do not be so conceited as to imagine that people are watching and listening to you to the exclusion of all others. Be too conscious of your dignity as a man or woman to feel that you can be made the subject of jest or ridicule; be true to yourself; be simple and natural, and you will feel at ease.

"Columbus," says Leigh Mitchell Hodges, " stalking into the presence of Ferdinand and Isabella like a country bumpkin, uncouth of speech and rude of action, would not have even gained their attention, much less the wherewithal to discover a new world. Yet he might have been quite as sanguine in his belief that another continent existed! Had Napoleon been uncivil and rough-spoken to his soldiers, they would not have followed him through all his changing fortunes to Waterloo, despite his genius and superb generalship. A boisterous and impolite Washington would never have been intrusted with the future of a struggling nation, no matter what ability he possessed. The men who have accomplished things in this world have, as a rule, been those who realised the value of politeness. The exceptions are few and far between—barely enough to prove the rule.

There has been no time in the annals of civilisation when good manners counted not for a great deal; and, in this day, when a man is so largely dependent on his personality for whatever of success and advancement he may obtain, their importance is doubly increased. Manners often place within easy reach what money cannot buy, and politeness has won more victories than powder."

When Edward Everett took a professor's chair at Harvard, after five years of study in Europe, he was almost worshipped by the students. His manner seemed touched by that exquisite grace seldom found except in a woman of rare culture. His great popularity lay in a magical atmosphere which everyone felt, but no one could describe, and which never left him.

The president of one of the largest banks in New York, in enumerating the essentials to success in banking, gives courtesy the first place. "If I could command the speech of twenty nations," he says, "I would preach politeness in them all. It is the Aladdin's lamp of success. I do not speak idly in praise of politeness, for, out of the experiences of fifty-six years in the banking business, it has been borne in upon me almost daily that courtesy is one of the prime factors in the building up of every career. It is the hall-mark of the Christian gentleman and of the keen man of affairs."

John Wanamaker attributes his prosperity largely to the just and courteous treatment of his customers.

The widely known grocery firm of Park & Tilford, perhaps the richest in the world, was started by Mr. Park in a small obscure store in New York. His pleasing manners and careful attention to customers attracted trade. His business grew rapidly, and Mr. Tilford, who was equally agreeable, became his partner. They made it a rule never to retain a clerk who betrayed impatience or petulance, or who failed to be as courteous to the poor woman whose purchases amounted to but a dollar, as to the richly gowned wife of a millionaire who drove to the door in a carriage, and ordered a hundred dollars' worth of goods.

When asked by what means he had contrived to accumulate so large a fortune, Zachariah Fox, the famous Liverpool merchant, replied: "Friend, by one article alone, in which thou mayest deal, too, if thou pleasest—civility."

The largest establishment in Paris, where thousands of clerks are employed, and where almost everything is kept on sale, was literally built up by the courtesy and politeness of its founders, Aristide Boucicault and his wife Marguerite. They started a little store on the spot where the immense Bon Marché now stands. Their invariable courtesy to patrons, and the constant efforts to please, soon attracted trade, and they added store after store until the great Marché resulted.

A good workman, says Robert Waters, had come to Mr. Blank for employment, at a time when the latter had no position to offer him. "But," said he to the workman, "I know where you can get work. Just go over the river to Mr. Johnson, of Ironmonger street. Tell him I sent you, and he will give you a job."

The man cast his eyes on the ground and looked disappointed. He then said, in a hesitating way:

" Mr. Blank, I am obliged to you for your kindness; but, the fact is, I am not in a position, just now, to make that journey."

Mr. Blank took in the situation at once. Putting his hand into his breast-pocket, he drew out a ticket, which he handed to the workman, with the remark:

" Here, John, is a ticket that will take you over there in half an hour. Go right away, and I'll guarantee you'll get the job."

John took the ticket, which was worth just seven cents, thanked the donor, and went. He got steady work at Johnson's shop.

Five years afterwards, John entered Mr. Blank's employ, and worked for him for some time. A strike was about to take place. The men in the other workshops were already out. Mr. Blank's men were about to follow, when John called them together, made an appeal to them to remain at work, and clinched his address by the story of their employer's kindness to him at a time of sore need. The speech saved the day.

" The men kept at their work," said Mr. Blank, " and enabled me to finish my contracts. Had they not done so, I should have been ruined. I have looked upon that seven-cent ticket as the main cause of my continued success in business."

The roughest and most ignorant, as well as the gentlest and most philosophical, are alike pleased and attracted by agreeable, courteous manners, and repelled by a rude, uncouth bearing. What excuse is there for treating the humblest or most insignificant being that walks the earth in a manner that, applied to ourselves, would hurt our feelings or arouse our indignation?

"Here, Tommy, give me a match," called a prosperously clad business man to a little shivering newsboy who had taken refuge in the vestibule of an office building. The man had stopped on his way out to light a cigar, but his last match had been blown out by the wind.

The boy stopped his cry of "Last edition—Evening News," and looked up at the speaker. "Say, mister," he said, "is that a demand or a request?" "A request, my boy, a humble request," laughed the kindly merchant, recognising the reproof in the little street arab's tones. "I guess I'll have a couple of evening papers, too," he added, as he took the proffered match. "Thank you. Here's a quarter, and you may keep the change." The lesson was needed, although the gentleman was not unkindly. He had simply failed to extend the law of courtesy to the poor boy. But the truly courteous man and woman, the gentleman and gentlewoman, makes no distinction. With them courtesy is no respecter of persons; it has no rank, because it should be found in all ranks.

Mrs. Grover Cleveland, whose exquisite manner and courtesy, aside from her personal charms, made her one of the most popular mistresses the White House ever had, made no distinction between her reception of women of fortune and the poorest in the land. One who witnessed the little scene, relates an incident characteristic of her unfailing courtesy and tact.

At one of the public receptions given at the White House, an old lady who was pressing forward, with those who were anxious to shake hands with the President's wife, dropped her handkerchief. She tried to recover it, but the eager crowd pushing from behind was too intent on its object to notice the old lady's effort to regain her property, and carried her along in the rush. Mrs. Cleveland's quick eye, however, noted the incident, and, stepping forward, she picked up the crumpled handkerchief, which had been walked upon by the crowd, and, tucking it in her dress, took her own fresh, dainty one of finest cambric and lace, and smilingly handed it to the old lady, with a pleasant " Please take mine, will you not? " as if she were asking a favour instead of conferring one.

A little girl, shy, timid, and ill at ease, sat at one end of the piazza of a large hotel, looking longingly at a gay group of children having a merry time at the other end. Neither she nor the aunt who sat beside her appeared at home in their new surroundings. They were not accustomed to meeting strangers. A bright little gentlewoman of ten, or thereabouts, left the noisy, laughing group, and went toward the newcomers. Taking a seat beside the younger of the two, she introduced herself, and asked her if she would not like to play with her and her companions. "I went once to a hotel with mamma," exclaimed the gracious little lady, "and nobody spoke to us. I remember how lonesome I felt, and, since then, I always speak to strange children." What timely thoughtfulness! What exquisite human sympathy! What a perfect adherence to the Golden Rule.

Little Archie McKay had none of the social advantages of this child, but he was animated by the same spirit, the spirit which makes a peasant the equal of a king. He was one of hundreds of little waifs who stood outside the door of a mission hall in Glasgow, one Christmas Eve, waiting for admission. They had assembled long before the appointed hour, so eager were they to see the beautiful Christmas tree and to partake of the feast to which they had been invited. The keen wind swept searchingly around the street corners, and the frost described beautiful patterns on the window panes, while a little girl, who seemed to feel the cold more than others, kept shifting from one bare foot to the other, vainly trying to impart some warmth to her shivering limbs. Archie, who had been watching her for some time, forgetful of his own discomfort, started forward; and, with a more chivalrous spirit even than that of the courtly Raleigh, when he spread his rich cloak beneath the feet of his royal mistress, the untutored Scottish lad placed his tattered cap at the feet of the little lassie, with the invitation, " ye maun stand on that."

A fine manner more than compensates for all the defects of nature. The most fascinating person is always the one of most winning manners, not the one of greatest physical beauty. The Greeks thought beauty was a proof of the peculiar favour of the gods, and considered that beauty only worth adorning and transmitting which was unmarred by outward manifestations of hard and haughty feeling. According to their ideal, beauty must be the expression of attractive qualities within—such as cheerfulness, benignity, contentment, charity, and love.

" A beautiful behaviour," says Emerson, " is better than a beautiful form. It gives a higher pleasure than statues or pictures, is the finest of the fine arts." We might go even further than this, and say that a fine behaviour actually, in a sense, makes the form beautiful; for is it not the expression of a fine, high soul, illuminating and transforming the body through which it gains utterance? To be sure, some are endowed with a rare charm of manner, a fascinating personality which no amount of drill in manners can impart, but nature has given everyone a capacity for being agreeable, courteous, and kind, and it depends largely on the training received in youth, and still more upon the exercise given this soul-germ as we advance from childhood to youth, and from youth to manhood and womanhood, whether it shall develop, sweeten, and strengthen our character, broaden our horizon, and enlarge our entire outlook on life, or shall die from neglect.

If young people starting out in life could be made to realise that good manners, courteousness, kindly consideration toward all—those below as well as above them in station—have more to do with success in life than a classical education, rank or wealth, self-interest if no higher or nobler motive, would urge them to pay more attention to the seeming trivialities of every day, the opportunities to bestow a kind word here and there, to do a little deed of kindness, to shed a ray of sunshine upon the path of some toiler by a word, or even a look, of sympathy. A simple "Thank you," a graceful recognition of any service, even though the doer be paid for his services, a soothing "I beg your pardon," for any unintentional annoyance or inconvenience caused others, undivided attention to those who converse with us, putting ourselves in the background and taking an interest in their affairs, patience to hear others speak, without interrupting, kindly consideration of the feelings of others, deference to the old, respect to all—these are some of the simple things which constitute what we comprehensively call " good manners." There is none so poor, none so ignorant, none so old or so feeble that he cannot put them in practice.

By example and precept, affable, courteous manners should be taught from the cradle upwards. If urbanity, politeness, and the utmost courtesy were practised in the home, if children were taught deference to parents, respect and reverence for the old, consideration for the rights and feelings of others, while their own were granted equal consideration, their natures would be so moulded that rudeness or discourtesy toward anyone, under any circumstances, would be in their eyes, as it is in reality, a sin against social laws and a violation of the precepts, " Love one another," and " Whatsoever ye would that men should do to you, do ye even so to them." The application of the Golden Rule to this as to every other question of ethics, would result in evolving a perfect system of conduct.

While grace of manner is not natural to all, it can, to a certain extent be acquired by observation, and by association with well-bred people. But civility, that true politeness which is the language of the heart, which "costs nothing and buys everything," may be shared in common by all mankind. It costs nothing; it buys everything— happiness in the home, harmony in the larger relations of life, and success in business.

II

'As a success winner, suitable and becoming dress is closely related to the matter of courtesy in conduct.

"Neither virtue nor ability will make you appear like a gentleman, if your dress is slovenly and improper," said General Lee, the leader of the Confederate forces, in warning a young man of the disadvantages of wearing a shabby coat. The warning applies with equal, if not greater force in these days of rapid work, rapid transit, rapid communication, rapid business methods. Employers of labour, busy men and women of the world, have not time to study minutely those who apply to them for positions; they are obliged to judge largely by appearances. Who can doubt, then, other things being equal, that the young man or woman neatly and becomingly dressed—not expensively or showily—will have a better chance of securing a position than the applicant who presents himself in shabby or slovenly attire?

The importance of attending to little details—the perfection of which really constitutes the well-dressed man or woman—is well illustrated by this story of a young woman's failure to secure a desirable position. One of those large-souled women of wealth in which our generation is rich, had established an industrial school for girls in which they received a good English education and were trained to be self-supporting. She needed the services of a superintendent and teacher, and considered herself fortunate when the trustees of the institution recommended to her a young woman whose tact, knowledge, perfect manners, and general fitness for the position they extolled in the highest terms. She was invited by the founder of the school to call on her at once. Apparently the young woman possessed all the required qualifications, and yet, without assigning any reason, Mrs. V. absolutely refused to give her a trial. Long afterwards, when questioned by a friend as to the cause of her seemingly inexplicable conduct in refusing to engage so competent a teacher, she replied: " It was a trifle, but a trifle in which, as in an Egyptian hieroglyphic, lay a volume of meaning. The young woman came to me fashionably and expensively dressed, but with torn and soiled gloves, and half of the buttons off her shoes. A slovenly woman is not a fit guide for any young girl." Probably the applicant never knew why she did not obtain the position, for she was undoubtedly well qualified to fill it in every other respect, except in this seemingly unimportant matter of attention to the little details of dress.

"A little bootblack upon the street," says Miss Lida A. Churchill, in the " Independent," " was, like his companions, ragged and out-at-elbows, but he was the proud possessor of a pair of shoes—and one day he conceived the happy idea of 'shining' them as an advertisement of his work. Very much impressed by their brilliant appearance, he was not a little mortified to find that the frayed and ragged edges of his trousers, which he had not noticed before, compared very unfavourably with his shining footgear, and he resolved that, if his advertisement were to have any effect, his trousers also must be 'shined.' When he went home that evening, he begged his mother to cut off the offending edges and put on a binding. The next morning, he felt a new sense of dignity as he sallied forth to his accustomed stand in all the glory of glossy black boots and neatly mended trousers. His satisfaction was marred, however, by the consciousness that his coat, greasy and out-at-elbows, and his tattered cap were not in harmony with his trousers. By

dint of close economy and the extra profits of increased business—the result of his improved appearance,—he saved enough to buy an entire new
suit of clothes.   The new raiment kindled higher
ambitions in the heart of the little bootblack.   He
must keep the pace set by his clothes, and he felt
they were superior to his work.   He must get
something to do more in keeping with them.   He
opened his heart to a friendly customer, and the
prosperous man, pleased with the boy's spirit, gave
him a place as a messenger in his establishment.
Years afterwards, when the ragged bootblack
had become the wealthy head of a large firm, he
attributed all his success to the effort ' to live up
to his boots.'   That lucky ' shine ' had made a
man of him."

It is true that clothes do not make the man,
but they have a much larger influence on a man's
life than we are wont to attribute to them.
Prentice Mulford declares dress to be one of the
avenues for the spiritualisation of the race.   Buffon, the naturalist and philosopher, testifies to the
influence of dress on thought.   He declared himself utterly incapable of thinking to good purpose
except in full court dress.   This he always put on
before entering his study—not even omitting his
sword!

III

A mother whose son was seldom at home of an evening, and who was made very anxious by this circumstance, appealed for advice to another woman whose boy could, as the mother declared, "hardly be driven outdoors after dark."

"How do you manage it?" asked the anxious visitor.

"Well," was the reply, "everybody with whom I am acquainted has to be managed through one or more of his five senses, and my experience with a brother, a husband, a son, and a daughter, has convinced me that the sense of and the conscious or unconscious longing for beauty and harmony is one of the most effective weapons to manipulate. When Tom began to go away evenings, I remonstrated gently with him. 'A fellow don't want to be always huddled up with the family, or to sit in a poky old cold room,' he answered. I thought a good deal about that answer, and, after awhile—for I didn't want him to think I was bribing him to stay at home—I had the fireboard taken down in his room, a grate put in, and a fire laid ready for lighting. I put down a bright rug, and hung up some pretty shades and two or three pictures. 'By Jove,' said Tom one day, 'I must invite some of the fellows in to see my swell den.'

"'Do,' I said. When 'the fellows' came, I sent up some cake and coffee served in my prettiest china. I kept the room fresh and bright and dainty, and Tom came to think that home was a better place than any he found outside, and to prefer it. Just fix up Harry's room so it will appeal to his sense of beauty, make him proud of it, let him do just as he pleases in it, and I'll warrant you'll bring him round."

Three months later Harry's mother reported to her friend: "Your plan worked like a charm. I almost wish Harry would go out now once in awhile at night, just for a change."

A cheerful, happy home life saved Harry as it had saved Tom.

Let youth be taught to look for beauty in all they see, and to embody beauty in all they do, and their lives will be both active and healthy.

Longfellow once gave to a young friend this advice: "See some good picture—in nature, if possible, or on canvas—hear a page of the best music, or read a great poem every day. You will always find a free half-hour for one or the other, and at the end of the year your mind will shine with such an accumulation of jewels as will astonish even yourself." To this good counsel another with greater wisdom adds: "Take into your heart every day some cheering word of God.

Listen to some heavenly song of hope and joy.
Let your eye dwell upon some beautiful vision of
divine love. Thus your very soul will become a
fountain of light and joy, and gladness will become more and more the dominant mood of your
life."

A writer in " Practical Education " speaks of
cheerfulness as life's " master-key." " In large
buildings," he says, " all the locks are under such
a system that one key, properly made, will unlock
them all. Such a key is called the master-key.
No room is closed to him who has the master-key.
He may go to any room. He may see all, know
all, enjoy all that may remain undiscovered to
him who has not such a key. The master-key
that unlocks more secret rooms for the teacher,
reveals more treasure than anything else, is a
sunny disposition. It opens the doors to more
hearts, young and old, than any other possession
that a teacher may have. The children love to
bask in the warmth of a sunny disposition. It
brings out their confidence."

What is true of the teacher is true of all who
have to deal with other lives.

" Are you happy? " a lady asked a city missionary. " I don't know," was the laughing reply.
" I have for the past few years been so busy trying to give other people help and sunshine, I
haven't had a minute to think whether I was

happy or not." But, as her face shone with a perfect radiance, one needed no further answer.

" Genuine pleasure," says one, " has this unique trait—the more you get for yourself, the more you provide for others." He might as truly have added that, the more you provide for others, the more you get for yourself. " It is a talent," said Ruth Ashmore, in one of her talks to girls, " which enables you to make more pleasant your surroundings; to make everybody eager to meet you and sorry to leave you; to give courage to the timid, to quiet unpleasant words, and to encourage agreeable conversation. What talent is this? It is composed, I think, of faith, hope, and charity, with love thrown in to leaven it, and patience added to increase it. When you possess it, not only will your life be a sunshiny one, but you will cease to be a homeless girl, and become a girl who makes a home wherever she is."

We all know remarkable people who have the wonderful faculty of turning common water of life into the most delicious wine. Some people turn everything they touch into vinegar, others into honey. There is something in the mechanism of some minds which seems to transmute the most sombre hues into the most gorgeous tints. Their very presence is a tonic, which invigorates the system, and helps one to bear his burdens. Their very coming into the home seems like the coming of the sun after a long, dark Arctic night. They seem to bring the whole system into harmony. Their smiles act upon one like magic, and dispel all the fog of gloom and despair. They seem to raise manhood and womanhood to a higher power. They unlock the tongue, and one speaks with a gift of prophecy. They are health-promoters.

Are we not coming more and more to recognise the importance of mental atmosphere, and the truth and significance of the assertion that "like attracts like?" Sunny-hearted, bright-faced people attract sunny people and sunny conditions. The human heart, like plants and flowers, turns instinctively toward the sun. Everyone wants a part of your joy; only as a duty or by a necessity will anyone share your gloom.

There is no situation, no condition, no state of mind, which will not be bettered and enriched by heart-sunshine.

CHAPTER XVIII

A COMPLETE AND GENEROUS EDUCATION

I call, therefore, a complete and generous education that which fits a man to perform justly, skilfully, and magnanimously, all the offices, both private and public, of peace and war.—MILTON.

A HALF-DEVELOPED human being is not a man; and, without a broad, liberal education, a man is not likely to develop all his faculties. Bishop Vincent has said that, if his son had chosen to be a blacksmith, he would still have sent him to college.

I do not think the question of how much money one can make thereby should influence his decision whether to go to college or not. It is simply a question of development, of whether the acorn wants to become a scrub oak or a giant among trees. In the greed for gain, many a boy has been taken from school and put into a store or office when he had scarcely acquired the rudiments of an education, seriously imperilling his chances of becoming a man. Hundreds of wealthy and prominent men would give half their wealth if they could go back to boyhood and get a collegiate training. A New York millionaire told me that he would give half his wealth for even a medium education. He said he had been put to work when a boy, without any chance to go to school, and that the lack of knowledge had mortified and handicapped him all his life.

Will an education pay? Will it pay a rosebud to unfold its petals and fling out its fragrance and beauty to gladden the world? Just as surely will it pay youth to get as liberal training as he can. No stunted life pays, when a larger and grander one is possible. The greatest problem of each individual is how to make life a glory instead of a grind—how to make even drudgery divine.

A successful lawyer in a large city, when speaking of his children, said: " I lie down at night afraid to die and leave to my daughters only a bank account." This man felt that there is something in the world greater than wealth, and that to bequeath to his daughters nothing but money, which might take wings, and the mere chance of a happy marriage, would be to leave them poorly equipped for life's battles. He felt that the mind should be emancipated from ignorance, in order to make his children citizens of the world.

It is a mean, low estimate of an occupation to regard it as a mere means of getting a living, without any thought of its influence upon the development of character, and its power to give that rich experience which elevates manhood and womanhood. It is an unworthy idea of a college training to regard it mainly from the standpoint of its mere commercial value.

"A man who has made the most of his opportunities, and who, in addition, has cultivated every faculty with which he is endowed," said Charles Dudley Warner, "has won success. It is the duty of everyone to make the greatest possible progress and to become as perfectly developed as ability permits. I believe every young man should go to college for the training he will get there. He is sure to come out better able to take his place in the world's work, and all his talents will be of greater use than if he had no training. I am afraid that there are few men who can say that they have made the most of their talents. We see the parable of the talents lived over again every day. The man who makes the most of what he has is the winner."

On the entrance gates to Cornell University, erected by President Andrew D. White, is the following inscription:

"So enter that daily thou mayst become more learned and thoughtful.

"So depart that daily thou mayst become more useful to thy country and mankind."

The student is more his own master at college

than in a fitting school. He begins to direct his own life, and to govern himself more than ever before. For a boy, it is an entrance upon manhood.

He begins at once to be educated by contact with other minds, acquiring self-knowledge by comparison. " College life is complex, a miniature of the larger world. The organisation of a college class; the election of its officers, the relations to other classes, the literary societies and fraternity houses, life in the dormitories, the debating unions, athletic exercises and contests, and the adjustment of work to recreation, bring into relief and develop the qualities of each student entering college. He meets teachers unknown before and new classmates, for the first time, thus laying the foundation of new and lasting friendships."

An education obtained in school and college, along with one's fellow students, is much better than that acquired by studying the same books and the same lessons alone, no matter how faithfully. Everyone who has tried it knows what an unsatisfying way it sometimes is to learn by solitary study. It can be done, but it is often more difficult than to learn in classes. College work has the stimulus and advantage of competition.

The class-room drill, the mental grapple between professor and pupil, and the game of give and take, serve as " eye-openers " to an earnest student.

" A college education," says President Charles F. Thwing, " stands for the investment of power. Each student invests power, and power he takes out; for education creates and increases power. Two things it specially promotes, which modern life demands; the power to think, and the power to will.   The power to think is the greatest intellectual power. The power of knowledge is the power of the granary, which gathers up and holds the harvests of many a field; the power of thought is the power of the mill which grinds these harvests into flour for the use of man. The power of thought is the power to see, to foresee, to reason, to judge, to infer. It is the power which every study of the college helps to train. Language gives discrimination, science, observation; analysis, synthesis; mathematics, also analysis and synthesis—the taking apart and the putting together of elements of thought; history, comprehension, and philosophy, self-repletion and self-discovery. In some ways—and the exact way is still unknown—the man who pursues these and the other studies of the college for four years becomes a thinker. When he entered college, he knew little, and could think less; when he leaves college, his knowledge is still limited enough; but he has gained a distinct power to think. This power to think is most urgently needed in the life of every person.   Ask the heads of the great corporations of the United States what is the quality which they most wish to find, and which, they learn, is the hardest to find in the men who come to them seeking employment, and the answer will largely be, the quality of being able to think.   He also becomes experienced in the control and management of men.   Through his relations with all the students, and especially through his interests in or work for the various associations of the colleges—athletic, social, scholastic—he is teaching himself to be an administrator, an executive.   A friend of mine who is the manager of a Utah mine at an annual salary of twenty thousand dollars, said recently: 'Harvard College, through its teachers, helped me much; but Harvard College, through its football team, helped me very much more.'   To him, scholarship was something, yet executive power was of greater value.   Ability to think clearly, largely, truly, and the power to will promptly, firmly, and with large intelligence, represent a mighty form of the investment in a college education."

"There is no doubt," says President Francis W. Patton, "that college training prepares a man for the big things of life better than any home training or plain business experience, all other things being equal.   It gives him a broader view, and enables him to see the inter-relation of things—to understand that nothing stands by itself."

"No man ever lived largely and helpfully in the world, who was not filled with an inspiring conception of his own times," says Seth Low. "If we would avoid the mistake of finding our ideals in the past, we must equally avoid the mistake of undervaluing the past. The Americans who will read the story of the constitution and the arguments by which it was urged for adoption upon the people, will see at a glance how deeply the experience of remote antiquity, as well as of more recent times, was drawn upon by our sagacious forefathers. They, more than any others to whom I can point, succeeded in combining the wisdom of the past with an intelligent prescience of our own times, infusing into their use of both a profound confidence. I assume that a college-bred man will have this acquaintance with the past, and this reverence for experience, in larger measure than those whose training has been of another sort. A college education ought to give to a man perspective by enabling him to estimate the present in the light of the past. It ought to strengthen his mind by exercising and disciplining his powers; and it ought to broaden his outlook, by enabling him to know something, at least, of many branches of knowledge."

Some knowledge of the world's best literature, the best thoughts, and the most notable deeds of mankind, and of the underlying motives which have actuated men in the onward and upward movement of the race, should be one of the acquisitions of a college student; and this is an invaluable asset.

"The distinctive work of a college is to develop thought-power in those who come to it for the education which it has to give," says ex-President Dwight of Yale. "It receives its pupil just as his mind is opening toward maturity—just as he is beginning to emerge from boyhood into manhood and is becoming, after a manner and measure unknown before, conscious of himself as a thinking man. The four college years carry him forward very rapidly in his progress in this regard. The possibilities of mental discipline are very large. The result to be realised is of very great significance. The youth is to be made a thinking man. He is to be made, according to his years, a wide-thinking man, with his intellectual powers disciplined for the efforts awaiting them. He is to be fitted to turn the working of his powers easily and successfully whithersoever they may be called to turn. Mind-building is the college business, and the aim the college has in view is to send forth the young man, at the end of his course, with his mind built—not, indeed, in the sense that there will be no change or development afterwards, in all the years which follow, but in the sense of complete readiness for the beginning of the educated life of manhood. The education of the college is the building process."

For a youth to gain the advantage of a college course is to have his mind stirred by the passion for expansion, to be dragged out of the narrow rut of ignorance and put in connection with the great minds in literature and art, to come into close contact with truth in nature, to feel the divine touch of science, to be brought into intimate relation with the entire universe, and to quench his thirst at the fountain of perpetual youth.

If for no other reason, a college education pays by the pleasure and happiness it brings into one's life. Who, that has ever tasted it, can ever forget the joys of his college course. No other four years in one's existence can compare with the four college years, when the student is brought into the most delightful association with others at the age when high ambitions and elevated ideals are not yet shattered or dulled by disappointment, or the unbounded faith in human nature shocked by violated pledges. It is the flowering time of life, when the imagination is alert, when hopes are bright and prospects for the future are tinted with vivid colours. Perhaps the greatest pleasure in life is the satisfaction which comes, at college, from the feeling of growing power to reach out into the unknown. College friendships alone would almost compensate for the cost of a course. Add to this the increased ability gained to cope with men and things, to overcome obstacles, to conquer one's place in life and compel the forces of nature to serve us, and who can estimate the value of such a course?

We speak of a college education as an investment of capital, time, and energy. "The student invests himself," says a wise teacher; "this is just what he takes from the investment; but it is a different self from the one which he put in. It is a self larger, finer, nobler, more symmetrical in the relation of intellect to heart, of heart to will, and of will to conscience; more aspiring, with greater power of achievement, more potent under difficulty, more quiet in triumph, more eager to do the best of which it is capable, and more determined to promote the rule of righteousness and to extend the realm of truth. Such a self-hood for each man, a college education represents. Too often the college fails to secure this noblest result in the personality of its graduates; but, to not a few of them, it is a mother, who has given not simply life, but has also, creating life in the student, nourished it into life eternal. Whatever may be in store for the American college as the predecessor of the American university, it can never cease to be an agency for the training of a man in the great business of living. It enriches his life; it deepens and broadens his view of truth; it ennobles his aims; it strengthens his choice of the right; it clarifies his vision of and his love of the beautiful."

This change from self to another self was thus expressed by Ruskin: ("Education does not mean teaching people to know what they do not know; it means teaching them to behave as they do not behave.") The mind of an educated man moves in "a broader and deeper channel which is always broadening and deepening as time goes on. When one learns what he did not know before, he becomes something he was not before. He is a larger man in every way, and has by just so much increased his capacity for happiness."

"That education which confines itself to mere learning," said Professor Asa Packard, "is of a very poor and unfruitful quality. What we all need, more than facts and figures, is courage, honesty, strength, a keen sense of honour, and a true sense of justice. The greatest, most important work of the present day is to build up character; to weave into the warp and woof of the mind the belief that, (in the language of Charles Kingsley) it is infinitely noble to do right, and infinitely base to do wrong. The most shining success in the world is not a great mill, nor a great railroad, nor a great mine, nor a great fortune, but a well-rounded and symmetrical manhood and womanhood." This is the work of mind-building at its best.

"If I were to have the choice of a hundred million dollars or the pleasure I had in my college days and the pleasure I have had as the result of my education," says Abram S. Hewitt, "I would quickly choose the latter. With an education, you can make money, but with money you cannot buy an education."

"How priceless is a liberal education!" exclaimed President McKinley, in an address in San Francisco. "In itself it is a rich endowment. It is not impaired by age, but its value increases with use. No one can employ it but its rightful owner. He alone can illustrate its worth and enjoy its rewards. It cannot be inherited or purchased. It must be acquired by individual effort. It can be secured only by perseverance and self-denial. But it is as free as the air we breathe. Neither race nor nationality nor sex can debar the earnest seeker for its possession. It is not exclusive, but inclusive, in the broadest and best sense. It is within the reach of all who really want it, and are brave enough to struggle for it. The earnest rich and the worthy poor are equal and friendly rivals in its pursuit, and neither is exempted from any of the sacrifices necessary for its acquisition. The key to its title is not the bright allurements of rank and station, but the simple watchword of work and study. A liberal education is the greatest blessing that a man or a woman can enjoy, when supported by virtue, morality, and noble aims."

CHAPTER XIX

KNOWLEDGE AS A PRACTICAL POWER

THE cultured hand can do a thousand things the uneducated hand cannot do. It becomes graceful, steady of nerve, strong, skilful; indeed, it seems almost to think, so animated is it with intelligence.

This is true on an international scale. The industrial superiority of the Anglo-Saxon nations is due chiefly to the scientific and practical nature of their methods of training the young for their duties and functions in life.

When Germany set out to rival England in producing goods for foreign markets, she did it by reorganising the lower schools, spending more money, conducting them more intelligently, and building up the popular mind. This plan has proved successful.

What is true of a nation is true of an individual. A writer who makes a specialty of advising those who earn a living by manual labour says:

"Education broadens a man's views, makes him more cognisant of his condition, implants self-reliance and determination, stimulates a desire for improvement, and teaches him to adopt intelligent measures to procure it."

Does education conduce to success in life? The late Professor Packard, founder of a great commercial school, said:

"The best equipped man is as a rule the successful man. It is so in business life. Educated men are always at the front. They take the largest share of the prizes, not only in political and professional life, but in the office and counting house as well. They are found in much more than their numerical proportion occupying the best positions in our great banking, insurance, transportation and manufacturing institutions. Intelligence and knowledge are in demand in every department of industry. The trained mind as well as the skilful hand will always find a market and can always get the highest wages."

"Those who contend that brains are no longer wanted in shops," says the "Money Makers' Magazine," "will no doubt be surprised at the statement that to-day a great many positions of good pay in all sorts of engineering industries are seeking for men to fill them. An agency that procures situations for technical men and the higher class of mechanics has on its books dozens of applications that it cannot fill. This shows nothing new. A really capable man is rarely out of a position. Then, the conditions of business are better than for several years, and comparatively few who want work are without it. It is

encouraging to men endeavouring to fit themselves for more responsible work to know that the
demand for quality is constantly growing, and
not only that there is to-day a wider field for the
bright, wide-awake man, the capable young en-
gineer, and the man with good ideas of design
than ever before, but that the field is continually
enlarging."

Not one word does this money-making editor
say of a continually enlarging field for young
men who are not bright, wide-awake, and hard
students.   There is no calling in life in which one
is not benefited, as to his earning power, by studious habits and the acquisition of such knowledge
as pertains to the higher positions in that calling.

In New York, a net income of fifteen or twenty
thousand dollars annually was earned by a firm.
But one of the partners, with rare foresight, concluded that the business was capable of large expansion if he could come into possession of certain technical knowledge.   Leaving his partner in
charge of affairs, he entered a university in Germany, and for four years applied himself assiduously sixteen hours a day, as one only will who
has a great object in view.   A few years later his
most sanguine expectations were realised.   He
became the leader in his particular line, and the
profits of the business were increased tenfold.

The prime object of education is power—

ability to cope better with men and things, to become more efficient in the great struggle for existence. True education increases a student's strength to grasp, to hold, to utilise—especially to utilise. Practical ability to meet issues, to solve difficult problems, is the test of power. It does not matter how much you know, how much theory you have stored up in your mind; if you cannot marshal your knowledge at will, and concentrate it upon the weak place, you are an impractical man and will not succeed. You must make every bit of your knowledge practical or it will not avail you in your success-struggle.

"A man is educated," says Minot J. Savage, "who is so trained in his perceptive faculties, in his analytical powers—so trained in all his abilities of one kind and another that, put him down in the midst of difficult surroundings, he will be able to see where he is, able to understand what the occasion calls for, and be able to master his conditions instead of being overwhelmed by them. The man who can master himself, and master his surroundings, wherever he may be,—only give him a little time,—he is an educated man. The man who is the victim of his conditions and surroundings, with no practical ability or power, may know ever so much, but he is not educated. Useless knowledge, then, is not education. Practical, live, and comprehensive command of one's abili-

ties, and the full development of one's native resources, constitute the true education."

Never before did the world call so loudly for
the practical, the sensible, the useful. Common-
sense is the genius of the age. In the great rush,
the actual is pushing aside theories and theorists.
On every hand, we hear calls for men who can
do things, not men who can philosophise about
them. The great interrogation point of this century is: " What can you do? " Not " What are
you? " " Where were you educated? "—but
" What practical things do you know? "

Learning is not wisdom, nor vital energy, nor
is it a substitute for common-sense. Knowledge
must be converted into faculty. Colton says: " It
is better to have wisdom without learning, than
learning without wisdom."

There has been no small amount of discussion,
in recent times, about how far college education
transmutes knowledge into power. And the practical youth is asking: " Will it pay to go to
college? " *Look about you.*
At the outset, examine the census. It appears
by this that ninety-two per cent. of our population
gain a livelihood by manual labour. Only eight
out of a hundred enter upon business or professional life. If your life work is that of one of the
ninety-two, and if elementary schooling is all
you can easily secure, there are open many paths

for acquiring more education, but a college course is rarely one of them. If, however, your life lot is to be with the eight in a hundred, it will pay to go to college, or to secure an advanced grade of technical training. Many of the colleges, to-day, have features in common with the great technical schools, and the technical schools with the colleges.

Many mere money-makers have succeeded well without an advanced education, and among them the theory often obtains that elementary schooling is enough, and that distinctively business training should begin at the age when a youth usually goes to college or to a preparatory school.

Let this be as it may, mere money-making is not the highest kind of success.

For him who aims to secure the highest development of his faculties, anticipates the joy of achievement, has a worthy life purpose, and makes it the grand goal of an educational course to fit himself for upbuilding society and the state, no course of schooling can be too extensive.

"As a rule," said Benjamin Disraeli, "the most successful man in life is the man who has the best information."

What a contrast there is between the cultured, logical, profound, masterly reason of a Gladstone and that of a hod-carrier who has never developed or educated his reason beyond what is necessary to enable him to mix mortar and carry bricks! The difference between the two is—carried back to its ultimate causes—a difference in education.

When I speak of eight men out of a hundred throughout the nation as engaged in the service of mankind, through advanced mental labour, I might speak of them as men of selected lives, set apart for the conduct of different affairs from those that commonly fall to those engaged in manual labour. In saying this, no disrespect is cast upon the eight or the ninety-two; it is the mere statement of a fact. Here we find eight men in the hundred who are to gain a livelihood by intellectual activity, in business or in professional life; such men cannot afford to do without a college course or the most advanced education that is obtainable. Their intellectual tendencies, their inborn leadership, will lead them to enroll themselves with those who seize upon the advantages offered by colleges.

William T. Harris, the United States Commissioner of Education, is authority for the statement that the chances of success, in respect to securing and holding the most influential positions in a highly civilised community, are, for properly educated persons, as two hundred and fifty to one over the uneducated. This statement is based upon an analytical study of name lists that comprise the most eminent citizens of the nation, in a cyclopedia of biography. President Thwing, I think, first published these statistics. These figures relate to former years during a considerable period of time, and include certain comparative statistics of population.

I have also seen another calculation based upon the per cent. of American youth who go to college, and the per cent. of leading positions that are at a given time held by college graduates, showing that two-thirds of the positions are occupied by perhaps only two per cent. of the population; that is, by the two per cent. most thoroughly educated.

A very wealthy man in one of the western States says: " I worked in the summer to earn money, and worked in the winter for my board, and studied. I went to school only one winter after I was fifteen years of age, but I was always studying books and men and things. If I had received a college education, I could have gone to Congress. I could have succeeded in many ways where I have failed."

A lawyer of considerable influence says: " I do not think there has been a day in twenty years that I have not felt the need of more education. By persistent hard work, I have acquired something additional to the schooling of early years, but I am far from contented with my outfit in this regard."

Someone has well said that the mental capacity

of a college graduate is like the power of steam
or electricity, which is not applicable to running
one kind of engine merely, but to any mechanical
appliance. " The untrained man makes one
think of Niagara going to waste, or only half util-
ised; or of a team of horses labouring through
mud and mire when they might haul tons on a
smooth road."

Harvey E. Fiske, the banker, in an article in
" The Outlook," on " The Value of a College
Education to a Business Man," says:

" I am a great believer in laying deep, broad,
substantial foundations for all undertakings in
life. . . . If a boy intends to become something more than an under-clerk or a small trades-
man, he will need the best preliminary education
that his parents can afford to give him.

" In the early stages of his career in business, a
young man will not appreciate what he has missed
by not going to college. Assuming that he entered
an office or a store at seventeen, and that his friend
entered college at the same age, he will feel at
twenty-one greatly the superior of his friend in
business ability. But five or ten years later, the
one who had the college training will probably be
found to be working more easily, with greater confidence, and with exactly as much success as the
friend who had four years the start—if not
greater. A college education will strengthen all

your faculties, and, rightly used, will be a blessing all through life."

"A college course," says a vigorous writer, "is called an 'education' through courtesy, I suppose. A college course is not an education—it is only the beginning of an education. It is the foundation, and it should be a good one, but it is for the student to build the superstructure during the rest of his life and by his own efforts. It is a fact which the student cannot too soon learn, that college training does not and cannot teach much more than the rudiments of a science or an art. Instead of educating a man, a college course merely prepares him to study intelligently. A diploma does not stand for a great deal of learning, after all—it is only a certificate that the owner has taken the stipulated course of study in the college which gave it."

The college is primarily a discipline, a mental gymnasium. It tests one's powers. It teaches him to think. Other things being equal, the college man will outmatch, as a business man, one of less mental training.

"If the sole object of life is to acquire wealth," says President Angell, "then no doubt many young men can attain that end as well without seeking the higher education. But if the young are to ask how they can best develop their manhood and how they can be useful to society, and if society is to ask what type of men can be most helpful to mankind, then there is no ground for fear that the number of students in the higher institutions of learning will decline, or that the general and final verdict will be that the proportion of them to our entire population is too great or is in danger of becoming too great."

I advise every youth to get a college education, whenever it is possible. The chances are that, if he makes proper use of the advantages it confers, he will be a happier, larger, and more useful member of society than he otherwise would be.

On the other hand, there is no doubt, from a practical standpoint, that there are some drawbacks to a college course. The methods adopted do not seem to develop practical ability, and do not always evolve the order of mind best calculated to win success. The theoretical, the speculative faculties, those which weigh and measure, and ponder and consider, and turn over and consider again, are often over-developed; while executive ability, which brings things to an issue quickly, which decides promptly and acts vigorously, is frequently undeveloped in the college man.

His training has not demanded of him prompt action, instantaneous decisions; he has had time to weigh and balance and consider, and perhaps to leave things undecided. But, when he gets into the work of everyday life, he finds conditions

confronting him constantly which require immediate decision and prompt action; he cannot wait
until next week or next month, for they must be
settled to-day.   Here is where the graduate is
often placed at a disadvantage until he has been
out of college long enough to gain practical
knowledge.

Our American colleges have modified the higher
education not a little in the interest of the practical demands of the hour.   Competition has compelled them to do this.   The industrial and the
commercial world are now better served by the
colleges.   An increasing number of college men,
relatively, are entering business instead of professional life.   At Yale there are twenty-five more
men to the hundred who are to engage in business
than some years ago.   About one-third of the
graduates become merchants, or they become industrial leaders.   The scholar or professional man
is no longer the typical college man; he is jostled
by the man of affairs.

Hard-headed, practical young men are often
greatly benefited by college discipline, and they
become most efficient factors in civic life.   " There
is," says Seth Low, " a natural tendency in college-bred men to feel that the learning which
comes from books is an essential element in a
complete equipment, but the experience of mankind shows that many other qualities are no less

essential. The hard common-sense, the practical wisdom of the men who make their way in the world without many advantages of education, are no less desirable elements in the government of the commonwealth."

The same thing is true of business affairs. The value of that good sense is multiplied, however, if a well-trained mind be joined to it. Men of what John Locke calls "roundabout common-sense," when thoroughly educated, not only make the most efficient all-round citizens, but also the most successful industrial and commercial leaders.

As a rule, great corporations seek college men, because, other things being equal, they will ultimately make better heads, better leaders; and this, notwithstanding the fact of the general impression that college men are not practical. The heads of such institutions know that, if a man is made of the right kind of material, a college education, although it may temporarily prevent the development of the practical faculties, enables a man to analyse well, and to grasp conditions very quickly. The greatest drawback to the young graduate is that he is too full of theories, too near his diploma to be of very great value; but, after the dream of his future greatness has faded a little, and he settles to business, he will adapt himself very speedily; and, when he once masters the details of a business, he will make rapid strides toward the top. He has learned in college how to think, how to marshal his mental forces; and, when he has learned the different phases of his business and how to apply his knowledge, he will be a stronger man than he would have been without the higher education.

"Education," says President Thwing, "is a great time-saver in a career. It represents the going back a few steps of the one who is to make a leap; it gives a spring, a buoyancy, and a swiftness and effectiveness. The four years which a boy spends in college help him to get into the great places in his chosen calling earlier, and probably to continue in them longer. I chance to know that one of the greatest retail houses in one of the greatest cities—the identity of which I cannot of course, reveal—has recently drawn up articles of partnership to cover the next fifty years. Among the articles of the compact is that every son of these partners shall serve an apprenticeship of five years; but it is added, every son who has had a college education may have this period of five years reduced to three. This instance possibly receives additional force from the fact that this house is composed of members of that race which, on the whole, furnishes the best merchants in the world—the Jewish; a race that has not been specially distinguished—despite many conspicuous exceptions—for its partiality toward the higher education. One of the great hardware firms of Cleveland is accustomed to say that, when a college graduate has been in its employ a fortnight, he is of as much value as a high-school graduate who has been in its employ four years; and, of course, after the fortnight, his value increases in a geometrical ratio. This remark of my Cleveland friend seems to me too strong, but I venture to give it as evidence of the claim that a college education is a good investment of time.

"About one-third of the graduates of many colleges are now entering business, and at least a part of the return of the investment made in college education, by those who enter business, should be made in money. Illustrations abound to prove that the financial returns received by college graduates, from their investment in a college education, are very remunerative. The graduate begins his business career at the bottom, and receives the wages which the lowest subaltern does and must receive, but he rises rapidly from the bottom, and, the higher he rises, the more rapid is his progress. Only last night a great manufacturer said to me, 'I am looking for a man to come into my office, to whom I can pay more than ten thousand dollars a year'; and, shaking his head, he added, 'I can't find him.' The place to look for men who are capable of earning ten thousand or fifty thousand a year is the list of the graduates of the American colleges of the last ten or thirty years. The Pennsylvania Railroad is taking many college men into the various departments of its service. The pecuniary rewards which these men will receive, in the next forty years, will represent a very high rate of compound interest upon the sum invested in an education."

" It is true," says President Schurman, " that there is an increasing, and, just now, an unusual demand for college-bred men in all walks of life. As to engineers—fifteen years ago the manufacturers of machinery had to be coaxed to take those pioneers, the Cornell men, into their shops and give them a chance. But where one went, many followed. In the class of 1900, every student in this branch was eagerly bid for two or three times over. One great electrical firm alone asked to be given the entire class. There is observable, too, a gradual increase in the call for college-bred teachers in the public schools, and this demand will grow by what it feeds upon.

" All this is but the sign and symbol of an increasing complexity and organisation in our civilisation. Rough-and-ready methods are going out, and the untrained handy man with them. In all directions, as expanding American manufactures and commerce come into competition with those of Europe, it is daily more obvious that the higher skill and intelligence, making the closest use of its resources, will win. Nowadays, to do the work of the world as the world will have it done, and will pay for having it done, requires that a man be trained in the exactitude of scientific methods, and that he be given the wide mental outlook and the special training which he can acquire in the university, and nowhere else."

"At this university," says President Angell, "we have not for some time been able, even with our very large chemical laboratory, to meet the calls upon us for well-trained chemists."

"There is a dearth of thoroughly trained men in all professions," says David Starr Jordan. "The more exacting the conditions, the greater the need. The thoroughly trained man, nowadays, must be a college man."

"There is, at present," says President Arthur T. Hadley of Yale University, "an unusual call for college-bred men in the various trades and professions—a demand so great that we are hardly able to meet it. This is a thing which always happens in years of commercial expansion. If we compare the times of prosperity with those of depression, we find that the variation in the value of invested capital is greater than the variation in the value of current product. A college-bred man has invested anywhere from two thousand to ten thousand dollars in himself. The value of that investment follows nearly the same laws as the value of a steamboat or a furnace. When there is an exceptional demand for service, he is the one who feels its benefits most fully. When there is no special demand and when everybody is striving simply to pay current expenses, he finds it impossible to make interest on the investment, unless possessed of special qualifications as a man.

"I think the increase of college-bred men in business and politics will go hand in hand with an increase in the standard of public service and public life. I suspect that it should be regarded as a result of political improvement, rather than as its cause. The existence of new administrative problems at home and abroad is likely to increase the need for men of broad views and thorough training. This must have its effect on the education of our public officials in the next generation."

"After ten years' experience in the business world," says ex-President James H. Canfield, "the college graduate will easily lead the uneducated business man, all things considered; but he will have an avocation as well as a vocation; and, while he will be successful, he will work to live, and not live to work.

"Some of the most successful business men I have ever known have told me that they preferred college-bred men because they were able to concentrate their attention upon a given subject; they were generally men of higher character, and of higher aims and ambitions than the untrained men, and all this tended to loyalty, faithfulness, and general success.   The fact that the railway corporations—of the West, at least—and great manufacturing companies are using more and more college men is exceedingly significant.

"A modern, well-equipped, up-to-date college or university, with its faculty all alive and alert and in touch with the great world about them, gives young men the best, the surest, the swiftest and the most complete preparation for any form of activity to which they may desire to devote themselves in later life."

President Thwing, in an admirable paper, calls attention to one point not always duly emphasised —that a college student puts his own personal work into his studies, and into all the conditions that make up his college life; but he takes out of the college far more than his own investment of time and work—he takes out of it the work which his teachers and comrades put into the college, and these elements are of far greater significance than his own individual work would be, if not thus supplemented.   He becomes in this way an organic part of a great guild of highly educated men, whose work for advancing the highest interests of mankind has been carried on during many centuries, upon whose roll are the most eminent names of all ages.

Great men reached the heights, for the most part, through an early education which not only gave them a good start, but also enabled them to progress more rapidly than others, and to reach greater positions than others.

Chancellor Day of Syracuse University, in referring to one's fitness for his life work, and the making or finding a position in which to do the work, says:

"The size of yourself and the thoroughness and genuineness of yourself will determine your orbit. A puff ball cannot sail through the orbit of Jupiter. All the diameters between the two are determined by the density, the quality of each star. Men talk about fortune and friends and many adventitious aids to success. There often is a mistake in what is success. But men of power and quality who are and have what the world wants cannot be suppressed. Launch a star and it will find the orbit of a star. There are infinite and unalterable laws upon which it may depend to find its orbit. But it must be a star. And it will make its own orbit by what it is. That will determine its relation to all other stars and the field of its own eternal movements."

The preparation of stars for their orbits and of orbits for their stars is closely connected with the highest ranges of mind-building work in the world's great universities. What one learns in his college days of language, of history, or the details of scientific study, may die out of memory; but the enriched and beautified life and the gift of power will endure forever.

CHAPTER XX
MORAL DARING

I SHOULD have thought fear would have kept you from going so far," said a relative who found the little boy Nelson wandering a long distance from home.

"Fear?" said the future admiral. "I don't know him."

When John Pendleton Kennedy, once secretary of the United States navy, was fifteen years old, the War of 1812 was under consideration, and he determined that, if there should be a war with England, he would join the army. One thought held him back; he was awfully afraid of the dark, having been terrified by ghost stories in his childhood. In order to cure himself of his fears, he used to go at midnight to an extensive forest near his father's house, and walk about until morning. This he did until he was as much at ease in the woods at two o'clock in the morning as he was in his father's garden after breakfast. Although at first he saw enemies and ghosts at every step, he persevered until even these startling experiences ceased to alarm him. When war was declared he went to the front.

"To understand courage," said Lord Wolseley, "one must have thoroughly studied cowardice in all its phases, and they are infinite; it is the most subtle of mental diseases."

In the first battle in which he was engaged he ran away, and all the rest of the regiment with him. So, too, it is said, Frederick the Great, one of the most valiant fighters the world ever saw, fled in a panic from his first battlefield.

It is difficult, perhaps, to define courage. Lord Wolseley, in writing upon it, speaks of it as "the mental correlative and equivalent of perfect physical health. "This virtue in man," he says further, "follows the same natural laws as obtain in the cases of horses and dogs; the better bred all three are, the greater will be their innate pluck. In the well-bred man, however, there is found another element of the highest value; the man proud of a brave father, or, still more, of a long list of brave progenitors, even if fate has been so cruel as to give him their blood and a timid disposition, will feel bound to sustain what is commonly called 'the honour of his name.'"

During our Civil War, as the story is told in the St. Louis "Globe-Democrat," Miss Reader, a girl of seventeen, boarded the steamer, *Des Moines,* bound for Fort Donelson, to bring back her brother, who had been wounded.

Five minutes before the boat pulled out, a

courier announced that the *Des Moines* was to go up the Mississippi River with several other boats and take a regiment of soldiers to re-enforce Colonel Mulligan at Glasgow, Missouri.

The boats reached Glasgow at half-past ten that night. The soldiers disembarked, leaving one company on each boat for a guard. While in the act of landing, the troops were attacked by the Confederates, and driven back to the banks of the river. Many were killed, and many more were badly wounded.

The attack struck terror to the hearts of the women on board the boats, and several of them swooned. But Miss Reader hastened bravely down the gangplank to the scene of carnage.

Putting her right arm around a wounded soldier, she led him up the plank into the cabin. Although bullets were still flying thick and fast and those on board remonstrated with her, she made twenty-two such trips to the shore, each time bringing back a wounded man. After the boat had cut loose from her moorings, Miss Reader assisted the surgeon, and induced the terror-stricken women around her to tear up everything they could find that would make bandages for the sufferers. All that night she stayed up, attending to their wants.

The supplies ran short, and rations were cut down. The young nurse had scarcely enough on which to subsist, **yet she** divided her single meal with others.

On the morning after the battle the boats, which had retreated and anchored two miles below, returned to take aboard the remainder of the dead and wounded. Then it was that, with the troops of the Twenty-sixth Indiana Infantry drawn up in order on the shore and the officers assembled on the guard over the steamer's bow, Colonel Wheatley presented the brave girl with a fine white horse, and the soldiers gave three cheers for the heroine of the battle.

Captain Fremont has told the story of Ensign Gillis, when he saw a torpedo coming toward the *Porter* during the Spanish-American war:

"That fellow Gillis has nothing in him but plain nerve. I have to watch him all the time, but that time he was too quick for me. The torpedo was coming slowly; if it touched, a bed under the water would be our doom. He had his shoes and coat off before I knew it. 'Don't do it, Gillis; she's got her war nose on!' 'I'll unscrew it, sir,' said the boy, and over the side he went, threw his arms around the torpedo, headed it away from us, and then began feeling for its business end. Well, the aircock opened, and the torpedo dived from the ensign's arms to the bottom." Gillis was a Naval Academy cadet but three years **before.**

A California Scotchman, McGregor, was one of the most argumentative of men, and one of the calmest. Early one morning, as he was returning home, he was addressed by a man who emphasised his words with a pistol:

" Throw up your hands! "

" Why? " asked Mr. McGregor, calmly.

" Throw them up! "

" But what for? "

" Put up your hands! " insisted the footpad, shaking his pistol. " Will you do what I tell you? "

" That depends," said Mr. McGregor. " If ye can show me any reason why I should put up ma hands, I'll no say but what I wull; but yer mere requaist wad be no justification for me to do so absurd a thing. Noo, why should you, a complete stranger, ask me at this oor o' the mornin' on a public street ta pit up ma hands? "

" If you don't quit gassin' and obey orders, I'll blow the top of your head off! " cried the robber.

" What? Faith, man, you must be oot o' yer head. Come, noo, puir buddy," said McGregor soothingly, coolly catching the pistol and wresting it with a quick twist out of the man's hand.

" Come, noo, an' I'll show ye where they'll take care o' ye. Hech! Dinna ye try to fecht, or I'll shoot ye! By the way, ye might as weel put up yer ain hands, an' just walk ahead o' me. That's it. Trudge awa', noo."

And so Mr. McGregor marched his man to the city prison and handed him over to Captain Douglass.

"It wudna be a bad idea to put him in a strait-jacket," he said serenely to the officer. "There's little doot but the buddy's daft."

Then he resumed his homeward walk.

Stephen A. Douglas, according to Tilley, was but twenty-eight years old when elected one of the judges of the supreme court of Illinois. Joseph Smith, the Mormon leader, was on trial. When it appeared that the evidence would not convict him, it was proposed by a mob to enter the court-house, seize Smith and hang him. A gallows was hastily built in the court-house yard, and a boisterous mob rushed into the court-room where the prisoner was about to be tried. "Sheriff," called out Judge Douglas, as the mob crowded toward the place where Smith sat, "Clear the room! The proceedings of the court are interrupted." "Gentlemen, you must keep order! you would better retire," said the sheriff, a small, weak man, trying to carry out the court's order. "Judge," said he, as the mob instead of retiring kept crowding toward the prisoner, "they won't go out, and I can't make them." Several of the ringleaders, stimulated by the sheriff's confession, jumped over the bar, and started to seize Smith. They were arrested by Judge Douglas's rising and calling out to a large Kentuckian, who stood six feet and a half: "I appoint you sheriff of this court. Select as many deputies as you require. Clear the court-house. The law demands it, and I as judge of this court command you to enforce the law, and preserve the peace." The suddenly appointed sheriff obeyed the judge's orders. Hastily calling upon half a dozen men to serve as deputies, he knocked down three ringleaders; his deputies pitched six more out of the windows, and in a few minutes the court-room was cleared of the mob, who, seeing the fate of their leaders, scampered out of the door. Promptness and intrepidity prevented a murder, and secured a fair trial to the prisoner. The judge, however, had assumed an authority which did not belong to him. As the duly appointed sheriff was present, he had no legal right to appoint anyone to act as sheriff. He knew that, before he spoke; but a moment's hesitation would have sealed Smith's fate. He took the responsibility, and met the emergency.

Courage was a marked trait in the character of Cyrus Hamlin of Constantinople. He came one day upon a Turk most cruelly whipping a Greek boy of ten. "Don't kill me!" shrieked the boy. Dr. Hamlin gave the Turk's head a blow with his walking stick, that made him stagger. Four or five other Turks then bore down upon the scene, seeking to arrest him—an infidel striking a believer. "I faced them boldly," said Hamlin, and said: "I will have every one of you arrested. I will go to the Kolook and get a Saptie. You saw him beating that boy, and knew that it was against the law; and you did not even say a word." They were very humble and went their ways completely cowed. Another day Hamlin saw a Greek drunkard beating his wife fearfully in the street. He was a man large enough to master Hamlin. "I rushed down upon him," says the missionary, "twitched him to the ground before he knew what had happened, pounded him, kicked him, and made him cry out 'Aman! aman!' When I knew my breath and strength would give out, I shook my fist at him and said: 'The next time, you brute, I will give you into the hands of the Turkish police.'"

Recently a score of boys were on their way to school in an eastern city, when a boy of sixteen among them began to tease a little fellow of perhaps twelve years.

Suddenly the annoyed smaller boy threw an apple core at his tormentor, whereupon the big boy pounced upon the little fellow, saying:

"I'll let you know that you can't throw apple cores at me! You take that!"

The little fellow shrieked with pain. He could

contend but feebly against his far larger and stronger assailant, and none of his schoolmates offered to go to his relief.

Leaning against a lamppost up the street was a typical street gamin, ragged, unkempt, and far removed from the tidy, well-fed and well-dressed schoolboys. Their life ways were far apart. A bundle of newspapers he had been unable to sell was under his arm, and he seemed to be looking about for a customer. Suddenly he let the unsold papers drop to the snowy ground and came running lightly and swiftly down the street, his blue eyes aflame and his grimy fists clenched. The next instant the big, well-dressed assailant of the small boy found himself seized by the collar and jerked violently to the ground by a boy of about his own size, who said, boldly:

"Take a kid o' yer size when ye want ter fight, ye big coward! Take a kid o' yer size! Touch that little kid ag'in, if ye dare!"

The big fellow struggled to his feet, and said, blusteringly: "Who's going to keep me from touching him if I want to?"

"I am!" said the gamin, standing as erect as a West Point cadet; and, whipping off his ragged jacket, he gave his head a toss, and said again:

"I am goin' to see that you don't touch him ag'in! If you want to fight, take a kid o' yer size, I tell ye! Try yer hand on me!"

"Humph!" said the big fellow, without, however, offering to touch the "kid of his size."

"Yer a coward, that's what you are!" said the gamin. "Ye don't dare touch a kid o' yer size!"

Nor did he. Mumbling and threatening, he walked off, with the jeers of his schoolmates ringing in his ears.

The street gamin went on his way also, unconscious, perhaps, of the fact that, in his bold defense of the weak against the strong, he had manifested a kind of heroism all too rare among the boys of the world.

We speak sometimes of the heroism of common life. There is an underlying element of courage that is manifest in everyday affairs, as a fire, a runaway, a mad-dog rush, when officers or bystanders disregard personal safety to save others. Courage manifests itself in the contest maintained by fathers and mothers against poverty or ill-health, in the unceasing struggle to educate their children, to give them a fair start in life. Such courage is as greatly to be honored as that of national heroes.

Nothing is to be crowned with a more sparkling diadem than moral courage. It is courage with a moral basis, put into play for moral ends.

"In writing of courage," says Lord Wolseley, "it is impossible to omit a reference to my friend and comrade, Charles Gordon. His courage was an instinct, fortified by faith in God and in a future life." It was this courage which armed Hamlin, which armed the street gamin in a quarrel not his own. "The greater part of the courage that is needed in the world is not of a heroic kind. Courage may be displayed in everyday life as well as on historic fields of action. The common need is for courage to be honest, courage to speak the truth, courage to be what we really are, and not to pretend to be what we are not, courage to live honestly within our means, and not dishonestly upon the means of others."

The man who is not true to himself, who cannot carry out the sealed orders placed in his hands at his birth, regardless of the world's "yes" or "no," of its approval or disapproval; the man who has not courage to trace the pattern of his destiny, which no other soul knows but his own, can never rise to the true dignity of manhood, or attain success.

"How much self-torture would Jean Jacques Rousseau have saved himself had he known the virtue of moral courage! How different would have been the fate of poor Goldsmith, that bright intellect and tender heart, had he the resolution to put aside his little vanities and extravagances! Moral courage would have saved Pope from a thousand petty follies. If we would but look stead-

'fastly to what is true and right, resisting every effort to divert us from the one straight path, we should not find ourselves struggling in quagmire and quicksand."

It takes courage for a young man or woman to stand firmly erect while others are bowing and fawning for praise and power. It takes courage to wear threadbare clothes while your companions dress in broadcloth and silks. It takes courage to remain in honest poverty when others grow rich by fraud. It takes courage to say "no" squarely when those around you say "yes." It takes courage to do your duty in silence and obscurity although others prosper and grow famous while neglecting sacred obligations.

It takes courage and pluck to be laughed at, scoffed, ridiculed, derided, misjudged—to stand alone with all the world against you. It takes courage to practise rigid economy while those about you squander their earnings, but "They are slaves who dare not be in the right with two or three!" It takes courage to refuse to follow custom when it is injurious to health and morals.

To espouse an unpopular cause often requires more courage than to lead a charge in battle. It takes courage to be true to yourself while others about you would rather strangle their individuality than be tabooed by Mrs. Grundy. But remember that all these things serve a brave soul, and the world makes way for the man who boldly presses on.

"If there be one thing upon this earth that mankind loves and admires better than another," said James A. Garfield, "it is a brave man—it is a man who dares to look the devil in the face and tell him he is a devil."

The moral courage of Gladstone, when a schoolboy, was shown by his turning his glass down rather than drink a toast of which he disapproved. If a man would accomplish anything in this world, if he would make his mark on his age, he must not be afraid of assuming responsibility. An incident is related of Gladstone in later life, which shows his perfect fearlessness in what he believed to be right—a quality which made him one of the colossal characters of his time.

Gladstone, as premier, presented a bill for Queen Victoria's signature to which her Majesty was decidedly opposed. She refused to sign. The premier argued with her, and endeavoured to convince her that it was her duty to attach her signature. Still she refused. Finally Mr. Gladstone, in his most courtly manner, but with much decision in his tone, said:

"Your Majesty, you must sign!"

The Queen instantly roused with indignation and exclaimed: "Mr. Gladstone, do you know whom you are addressing in this manner? I am the queen of England."

"True, your Majesty, but I am the people of England, and you must sign!"

This she finally did; and time proved the necessity and justice of his demand.

At Stockholm, Jenny Lind was once requested to sing at the king's palace on Sunday, at some great festival. She refused, and the king called personally upon her and commanded her to sing. "There is a higher king, sire," she replied, "to whom I owe my first allegiance."

General Gordon's almost magical influence arose from the all-pervading sense, inspired by his mere presence, that here was a man who always was, and always would be, inflexibly true to his highest conviction. When he was in the Soudan, he never hesitated to place outside his tent the white handkerchief, which meant, as all men knew, that he was at prayer, and that, during that sacred hour when he was alone with God, he must not be disturbed.

What is nobler in manhood than standing inflexibly by one's sense of right, standing by heaven and its beneficent laws, whether or not the earth approves.

When a phrenologist examined the head of the Duke of Wellington, he said: "Your grace has not the organ of animal courage fully developed."

"You are right," replied the great man; "and I should have retreated in my first fight but for my sense of duty."

"Duty is far more than love," says Mrs. Jameson. "It is the upholding law through which the weakest become strong, without which all strength is unstable as water."

"It is not what a lawyer tells me I may do," says Burke; "but what humanity, equity, and justice tell me I ought to do that governs my conduct and action."

It is this great underlying law of life—that sense of duty to God and humanity upon which the Iron Duke's courage was based and which has guided the great leaders of our English speaking race—that is the secret power underlying all that is most beautiful in the moral life of our age.

"Don't you know your own life is in danger?" said Mary A. Livermore to a beautiful young Sister of Mercy, who seemed to take no thought for herself while with unwavering devotion she attended the plague-stricken sufferers in a great city.

"Yes," replied the Sister, gently raising her brown eyes to meet her questioner's gaze, "I know it is; but I would rather die doing my duty than live and know that I had not done it."

CHAPTER XXI

LOVE—THE TRUE GLORY OF LIFE

THE history of the progress of the working classes in this century in England," said Salisbury, " is very largely the history of one man's life—that of Shaftesbury." Mr. Gladstone's tribute to the work of the great reformer was in part expressed in these words: " The safety of our country is not in law or legislators, but in Christian gentlemen like unto Lord Shaftesbury."

Very early in his career, this favoured child of rank and wealth entered the lists as a champion of the poor and oppressed. Turning aside from the allurements of his high station, from paths of ease and pleasure, he followed his ideal wherever it led, no matter how rough the road, or how bitter the opposition he encountered. To raise the social level, to improve the condition of poor working men and women, became the mainspring of his existence, and to this he devoted himself with unwearying devotion for over half a century. How he succeeded is now a matter of history.

" Ragged " schools, evening and day schools, " model " tenements, " shelters," clubs, reading-rooms and coffee houses replaced, as if by magic, the foul dens and vicious resorts which, thitherto, had been the homes and places of entertainment of the multitudes of London poor whom he succeeded in reaching. Costermongers, bootblacks, newsboys, shopwomen, seamstresses and working girls, factory employees, men and women in the manufacturing districts of England, workers all over the country, regarded him as a messenger from heaven. When his labours were ended, the whole nation mourned. Rich and poor, high-born and low-born alike, followed his earthly remains to Westminster Abbey. Royalty, lords, commons, merchants, statesmen, scholars, factory hands, seamstresses, flower girls, chimney sweepers, costermongers, labourers from east and west, north and south, by hundreds of thousands, as members of one family, wept over his grave as for a beloved father.

" The whole sum of this title of life is service," said Phillips Brooks—" service to others and not to self. Self is a narrow space. I wish to speak to the young men who have just opened the door of life, and to the old men who are just before the door that opens to a life beyond. Life is not an existence for self. It is this service that is the grand exponent of a successful life. To determine what success a life may attain is to see how much a life may accomplish for the bettering of humanity. I wish I had the power to convince every one of my hearers of the importance of service. In service you throw yourself into another life. The other life becomes part of yourself, you part of that other life; you are one. You work together for the bettering of the world. Just so you enter into God and the divine life enters into you. You do not surrender to pope, priest, or church, but still have your own independence. You simply surrender to God. To make life as successful as you can, you should not go away by yourself and say that you will live a good life, and then do nothing else. To cherish self is not the way to do service. You must lose self. Make yourself so strongly a part of the whole world that you influence all the other parts, and more strongly cement them together. Take in some other life. Serve it and show it that there is a divine image hidden in it. Develop that image, and in so doing you benefit your own life. . . . . No man has come to true greatness, who has not felt in some degree that his life belongs to his race, and that what God gives him, He gives him for mankind."

Call it by what name you will—charity, benevolence, philanthropy, unselfishness, brotherhood of man—it does not alter the fact that it is love—of which all these are varying expressions —that accomplishes the greatest work of the world, the work that raises man to his highest estate, and removes him from kinship with the lower animals.

Science has accomplished marvels, has disclosed to our wondering eyes a new heaven and a new earth, has harnessed the forces of nature in obedience to man's will, has tunnelled mountains, diverted the courses of rivers, annihilated distance, and brought continents thousands of miles apart, separated by mighty oceans, into daily communication. But it is love, with its purifying, elevating influence, that has laid its touch on man's heart, and bidden him, in the midst of the triumphant march of progress witnessed by the nineteenth century, hold out its hand across the world to the poor, the sick, the sorrowing, the suffering of every race, in every clime, to lift them up to participation in the advantages with which advancing science and the growing intelligence of mankind have blessed the world.

"And now abideth faith, hope, love, these three," wrote St. Paul; "but the greatest of these is love." The perfect character is based upon love—love to God, and love to one's neighbour. This is the fulfilling of the law, the attainment of the successful life.

"The spectrum of love has seven ingredients,"

says Henry Drummond, in his analysis of love according to St. Paul; " patience, kindness, generosity, humility, courtesy, unselfishness, sincerity— these make up the supreme gift, the stature of the perfect man. You will observe that all are in relation to men, in relation to life, in relation to the known to-day and the near to-morrow, and not to the unknown eternity. We hear much of love to God; Christ spoke much of love to man. We make a great deal of peace with heaven; Christ made much of peace on earth.

" ' The greatest thing a man can do for his heavenly Father,' it has been said, ' is to be kind to some of his other children.' I wonder why it is that we are not all kinder than we are? How much the world needs it. How easily it is done. How instantaneously it acts. How infallibly it is remembered. How superabundantly it pays itself back—for there is no debtor in the world so honourable, so superbly honourable as love. ' Love never faileth.' Love is success, love is happiness, love is life. ' Love!' I say with Browning, ' is energy of Life.' . . .

" You will find as you look back upon your life, that the moments that stand out, the moments when you have really lived, are the moments that you have done things in the spirit of love. As memory scans the past, above and beyond all the transitory pleasures of life, there leap forward those supreme hours when you have been able to do unnoticed kindnesses to those round about you, things too trifling to speak about, but which you feel have entered into your eternal life. I have seen almost all the beautiful things God has made; I have enjoyed almost every pleasure that He has planned for man; and yet, as I look back, I see standing above all the life that has gone four or five short experiences when the love of God reflected itself in some poor imitation, some small act of love of mine, and these seem to be the things which alone of all one's life abide. Every other good is visionary. But the acts of love which no man knows about, or can ever know about— they never fail. . . .

"In the heart of Africa, among the great lakes," continues Drummond, "I have come across black men and women who remembered the only white man they ever saw before—David Livingstone; and, as you cross his footsteps in that dark continent, men's faces light up as they speak of the kind doctor who passed there years ago. They could not understand him; but they felt the love that beat in his heart." Nothing else is remembered so long or so gratefully as kindness.

"Did you really intend to brave the terrors of the ocean in so frail a skiff?" asked Napoleon of a young English sailor who had escaped from captivity in the interior of France, reached the coast near Boulogne, and constructed a little boat of the branches and bark of trees, in which he was about to venture upon the stormy English Channel, hoping to be picked up by some British cruiser.

"If you will but grant me permission," said the youth, "I will embark immediately."

"You must doubtless, then, have some sweetheart to revisit, since you are so desirous to return to your country?"

"I wish," said the sailor, "to see my mother. She is aged, poor and infirm."

"You shall see her!" exclaimed Napoleon, energetically, "and present to her from me this purse of gold. She must be no common mother who can have trained up so affectionate and dutiful a son." Soon afterwards, he sent the young man in a French cruiser, under a flag of truce, to a British vessel.

Love is the golden key wherewith all hearts are opened. It is the magic door through which we must pass to success in work and life. Into everything you do you must put this mighty, vivifying force, or you will not succeed on the highest plane. You may go into the slums of a large city, or out into the highways and byways, through a sense of duty, or because you are a church member and do not wish to appear behind others, or for some other reason, to relieve the necessities of the poor, to instruct the ignorant and lead them to a knowledge of better things; but if you do not love the work, do not love the people you are trying to help, your efforts will be futile. " We love them first," said a member of the Salvation Army, in answer to one who had asked as to what their initial step was in endeavouring to reclaim the poor outcasts whom they rescue from the streets. This is the secret of the marvellous growth of the Salvation Army.

Whatever your occupation or profession, wherever your lot be cast, if you bring not love into it, life will be a dreary, hopeless failure. The truly successful teacher, for instance, is not the one who works for salary only, who maintains discipline by fear, and compels her pupils to study because they are afraid of the punishment that will be meted out if they do not; but the one who is anxious for their highest welfare, whose heart is in what she is doing, who tries in a general way, at least, to reach the higher springs of the lives she is so largely helping to mould. Love multiplies power; it is intuitive and has a way of reaching down to the heart of things impossible to the soul not guided by it. The clergyman who would succeed must be controlled by the desire to make men better; he must love, or he will never uplift them. A truly successful lawyer must not only love the law, but he must love truth and justice more; he must be concerned more for the interest of his client than for his fee or the reputation he hopes to win.

"When I was in the law school at Yale," says Conwell, "there was one poor young fellow there. A ragged boy he was. I loved that boy, though I had but little association with him. But I loved him because he was ragged and poor, and I would not be surprised if he loved me for the same reason. Many years have passed since then. While he was in the law school he was determined to be a judge. That was his fixed purpose. His father was opposed to it, and would not permit him to take from home anything but the clothes he wore. He worked and laid up a few dollars. He worked out of hours to secure his education. As he could not attend all the classes on account of his work, his friends in the college would help him. They would take notes of lectures and read them to him. He loved the law. He was fascinated with the idea of being a lawyer. He loved justice, he loved truth. When people saw his determination, they would say, ' He will succeed.' Now he goes his way into one of the highest places in the land. He has won it, not because he had anyone to help him, but because his love for the work was strong enough to win it."

The spirit which actuated this poor ragged boy —love of the work, and longing for truth and justice, with an unselfish desire to be a helper in the gathering movement toward community of interests or the brotherhood of man—are the surest means to win success in any career. It matters not whether you elect to be a scientist or a lecturer, a physician or a shipbuilder, a farmer or a mechanic, a teacher or a nurse, in no other spirit can you give to the world the best of which you are capable. If you have no other object than the advancement of your own interests, then will you miss the true joy of life.

"You talk of self as the motive to exertion," says Whyte Melville; "I tell you it is the abnegation of self which has brought out all that is noble, all that is good, all that is useful, and nearly all that is ornamental in the world."

What but an all-pervading love led Florence Nightingale to give up her luxurious home, her loving friends, all that conduces to personal comfort and happiness, to risk health and life on the battlefield and in the cholera-stricken camps of the Crimea?

At the battle of Fredericksburg in our Civil War, hundreds of Union soldiers lay wounded on the field a whole day and a night; the agonising cries for water among the wounded were answered only by the roar of the guns. At length a Southern soldier who could not endure these piteous cries any longer begged his general to let him carry water to the suffering. The general told him it would be instant death to appear upon the field, but the cries of the unfortunates drowned the roar of the guns, to him at least, and he rushed out among the wounded and dying with a supply of water on his errand of mercy. Wondering eyes from both armies watched the brave fellow as, heedless of guns, he passed from soldier to soldier, gently raising his head and placing the cooling cup to his parched lips. The Union soldiers were so deeply impressed by the action of this boy in gray, risking his life for his enemies' sake, that they ceased firing for an hour and a half, as did the Confederates. During this whole time the boy in gray went over the entire battlefield, giving drink to the thirsty, straightening cramped and mangled limbs, putting knapsacks under the heads of sufferers and spreading coats and blankets over them as tenderly as if they had been his own comrades.

"Before the birth of love," said Socrates, "many fearful things took place through the empire of necessity; but when this god was born all things arose to men."

It is because love is yet in its infancy that so many "fearful things" continue to take place in the world. It is because mankind is still in its childhood, the childhood of fear, of anger, of hatred, of restlessness, of selfishness and egotism, that men are base enough to trade upon the necessities of their brothers, that they may pile up money which they cannot use. Men speak evil, one against another, because they have not yet learned what love is. The law of love is service, but the chief aim of the self-seeker, the avaricious, is to be ministered unto rather than to minister. If the meaning of love were understood, there would be no wars, no hatred, no ill-will, no desire to outreach others; all base passions would shrink abashed before this divine power.

Love is the constructive force of the universe. Wherever found it is engaged in the work of building up lives, putting joy and beauty into their structure. Shielding the unfortunate, raising up the fallen, bringing new hope to the despairing, new light to dull and leaden lives, ministering to the sick in mind and body, smoothing the way for the tender and the footsore wayfarers on life's rough road, it goes through the world, a ministering spirit—ministering while it teaches men how to live.

In a country cemetery, a simple white stone marks the grave of a little girl, and on the stone are chiselled these words: " A child of whom her playmates said, ' It was easier to be good when she was with us.'" These few words tell the beautiful story of the short life. The child loved. Christ loved. That was the secret of the only perfect life. Love's influence for good is compelling. No matter how low a man may have fallen, it yet has power to raise him. He cannot resist its call even if he would. The soul of Mary Magdalen was moved to repentance by the love of Christ, and the sinner became a saint. Jean Valjean, Victor Hugo's immortal hero, driven to crime and desperation by the wrongs inflicted upon him by society, was won back to manhood through the love of the good Bishop Bienvenue, became wealthy and devoted his after-life to the service of humanity. Labouring in the convict prisons of England, Elizabeth Fry brought renewed hope and courage and long-forgotten impulses to good to the lives of many of the unhappy inmates who, perhaps, had never known what love is until this good Samaritan came to minister to them. What Christlike love she had for them is witnessed by her answer to a lady companion, who, noting that she was greeted affectionately as a familiar friend by the occupants of the women's cells in Newgate, inquired of what crimes they had been convicted. " I do not know," replied Mrs. Fry; " I have never asked them that. We all have come short." In our own day, Maud Ballington Booth is winning anew to self-respecting manhood and womanhood, and a place among the ranks of the world's workers, men and women who, but for her, would be driven back by a phar-

isaical society to those very crimes for which the
state undertook to punish them.

Some of the noblest philanthropies of modern
times have had their origin in the love of the poor
for the poor.

"Fifty years ago" says a recent writer, "a
young curate in Brittany had an idea. He himself had no money to further it, for his salary was
only eighty dollars a year, and his only friends
were the wretched. His idea was so simple as to
be almost ridiculous; it was that the poor should
help the poor. The enthusiastic curate appealed
to three women to help him. Two of these were
seamstresses and the other worked out as a servant. These four people agreed to pool their
wages and begin the new enterprise.

"So, in a poverty-stricken street in St. Servan,
the order of the Little Sisters of the Poor was
organised, and in a wretched attic the first pen-
sioners, two old women, were tenderly cared for.
Jeanne Jugan, the servant girl, was the first alms-
gatherer of the society.

"Inspired by a poor curate, undertaken by the
lowliest of people, beginning in a single attic room
in a rude tenement, one of the most remarkable
of the religious and philanthropic movements of
modern times was born. Christ had no humbler
origin. To-day the order has two hundred and
fifty houses on the Continent of Europe, and it

gives food and shelter to more than thirty-three thousand aged and poor people daily.

"The Little Sister with her basket or her cart is a familiar sight in large cities across the water, and the Abbé Le Pailleur has lived to see his noble dream extended beyond his prophetic vision.

"About two years ago a dressmaker, Annie McDonald, died in New York, and left her whole property, amounting to two hundred dollars, as a legacy to start a home for crippled children. Almost every other variety of charity had been attended to, but the crippled child, of whom there are so many in the rushing city, had been overlooked. To the dressmaker came the thought of this new charity for this old form of helplessness, and she left her fortune of two hundred dollars for this purpose with the trustfulness of one who was bequeathing twenty thousand. Thus the Daisy Fields Home came into existence. Back of the famous Palisades, not far from the Hudson River, in the middle of a broad field which is as white in summer with daisies as it is in winter with snow, stands the little hospital which fills a place that no other hospital has made any attempt to fill. There crippled children are taken, and from there they are not sent away. They are permanently sheltered until they are either cured or amply able to support themselves without pain.

But for the poor, lame teacher, Sophie Wright,

New Orleans would have no free evening school
for men and boys. When only sixteen years old,
Miss Wright, who had been self-supporting since
the age of twelve, saw the crying need of educational opportunities for the men and boys of New
Orleans who are occupied during the day. Failing in her attempt to get the public schools of the
city to receive these unfortunates in the evening,
she threw open her own doors to them; and after
teaching all day for a livelihood, she taught, for
love's sake, at night. She called for volunteer
teachers to help her in this work, and her call met
with response. Her school has grown until there
are now over one thousand men and boys in
attendance. Fathers and sons, men fifty years of
age and tender little lads, sit side by side in the
same class. The one requirement for admission
is the positive statement that the applicant is too
poor to pay a cent, and wants to learn and to improve himself. Many men and boys come bare-
foot. As far as she can, the teacher buys them
shoes, also books. Through the generosity of
kind friends, she has been enabled to enlarge the
scope of her enterprise, year by year, until her
schedule of classes includes painting, drawing,
clay modeling, music, and full courses in book-
keeping and other clerical occupations.

Everyone is familiar with the story of the Ger-
man-English philanthropist, George Müller, who,

in the early half of the nineteenth century, opened the famous Orphan House at Ashley Downs, England. He had no money to start the enterprise, but his love for the poor, homeless orphans, inspired a boundless faith that God would prosper the undertaking. This great institution, the product of one man's love and faith, which has educated and provided for so many thousands of waifs, is supported entirely by voluntary contributions.

Those royal souls who gave no less a gift than themselves realised the truth of O. B. Frothingham's words: " Begin with a generous heart. Think how you can serve others. Then shall you find resources to grow. Your own portion shall not be left desolate. Strength shall be shed through you. Do the utmost with what you have and it shall go far enough."

" Write your name with kindness, love, and mercy on the hearts of those with whom you associate, and you will never be forgotten." A Shaftesbury, a Cooper, a Peabody, or a Müller needs no bronze or marble monument to commemorate his name. The memory of our philanthropists is graven on the heart of the nations. Their works form their most enduring monument, and their names, handed down from generation to generation, will be emblazoned forever on the roll of the world's benefactors."

" Ye shall know them by their fruits."   A life filled with the fruit of kindly deeds is the only one that will find favour with God.

A holy hermit, as the legend runs, who had lived for sixty years in a cave of the Thebaid, fasting, praying, and performing severe penances, spending his whole life in trying to make himself of some account with God, that he might be sure of a seat in Paradise, asked him to show him some saint greater than himself, in order that he might pattern after him to still greater heights of holiness.   The same night an angel came to him and said:

" If thou wouldst excel all others in virtue and sanctity, strive to imitate a certain minstrel who goes begging and singing from door to door." The hermit, much chagrined, sought the minstrel and asked him how he had managed to make himself so acceptable to God.   The minstrel hung down his head and replied:

"Do not mock me, holy father.   I have performed no good works, and I am not worthy to pray.   I only go from door to door to amuse people with my viol and my flute."

The hermit insisted that he must have done some good deeds.   The minstrel replied, " Nay, I know of nothing good that I have done."

" But how hast thou become a beggar?   Hast thou spent thy substance in riotous living?"

"Nay, not so," replied the minstrel. "I met a poor woman running hither and thither, distracted, because her husband and children had been sold into slavery to pay a debt. I took her home and protected her from certain sons of Belial, for she was very beautiful. I gave her all I possessed to redeem her family, and returned her to her husband and children. Is there any man who would not have done the same?"

The hermit shed tears, and said that in all his life he had not done so much as the poor minstrel.

"I have come to see life," says Howells, "not as the chase of a forever impossible personal happiness, but as a greed for endeavour toward the happiness of the whole human family. There is no other success." This is but the interpretation of Christ's words: "He that findeth his life shall lose it; and he that loseth his life for my sake shall find it." The self-absorbed man or woman, the one who has never felt the thrill of human sympathy, the uplift of soul that follows a kind act, has missed the supremest joy that can come to mortal. George W. Childs, who used his honourably acquired wealth as a fund entrusted to him to be administered for the benefit of others, said, "If asked what, as the result of my experience, is the greatest pleasure in life, I should reply, 'Doing good to others.'" On another occasion he said: "I believe that children should

be educated to give away their little all; to share
their possessions with their friends; if they are
trained in this spirit, it will always be easy for
them to be generous; if they are not, it will be
more natural for them to be mean, and meanness
can grow upon a man until it saps his soul."

"Human beings," says Ruskin, "owe a debt
of love to one another, because there is no other
method of paying the debt of love and care which
all of us owe to Providence."

If you have no other gifts, you can be lavish
with kind words and acts. These cost nothing,
and, besides giving pleasure to others, enrich and
beautify your character as nothing else can.

To Artabazus, a courtier, Cyrus gave a cup of
gold, but to Chrysanthus, his favourite, he gave
only a kiss. Thereupon the courtier said, " Sire,
the cup you gave me was not so good gold as the
kiss you gave Chrysanthus." It is love that the
human heart hungers for in every age, and in
every station. Kind words and sympathy often
do more good than material gifts.

Alms-giving, so-called charity, without love, is
shadow without substance. It fails of its object,
and hurts both giver and receiver. " And though
I bestow all my goods to feed the poor," says St.
Paul, " and though I give my body to be burned,
and have not love, it profiteth me nothing."

Love is regal in its kindness and courtesy. " It

cannot behave itself unseemly. You can put the most untutored persons into the highest society and, if they have a reservoir of love in their hearts, they will not behave unseemly. They simply cannot do it. Carlyle said of Robert Burns that there was no truer gentleman in Europe than the ploughman-poet. It was because he loved everything—the mouse and the daisy, and all the things great and small that God has made. So, with this simple passport, he could mingle with any society, and enter courts and palaces from his little cottage on the banks of the Ayr."

Love is royal in its attributes, and it lifts all who embrace it to its own exalted level. It is the only thing that can bring true happiness to king or peasant. Hovels with this radiant inmate are palaces; palaces, without it are hovels. In a burst of spiritual fervour, Thomas à Kempis exclaims: "Nothing is sweeter than love, nothing more courageous, nothing higher, nothing wider, nothing more pleasant, nothing fuller or better in heaven and earth; because love is born of good, and cannot rest but in God, above all created things."

THE END

CPSIA information can be obtained at www.ICGtesting.com
Printed in the USA
LVOW09s1544150816

500456LV00007B/339/P